Steps to Freedom

First published in 2018 by
Liberties Press
1 Terenure Place | Terenure | Dublin 6W | Ireland
Tel: +353 (0) 86 853 8793
www.libertiespress.com

Distributed in the UK by
Turnaround Publisher Services
Unit 3 | Olympia Trading Estate | Coburg Road | London N22 6TZ
T: +44 (0) 20 8829 3000 | E: orders@turnaround-uk.com

Distributed in the United States by
Casemate IPM | 1950 Lawrence Road | Havertown | Pennsylvania
19083 | USA
T: (610) 853 9131 | E: casemate@casematepublishers.com

2 4 6 8 10 9 7 5 3
A CIP record for this title is available from the British Library.
Cover design by Roudy Design
Printed in the EU by Grafico

Steps to Freedom

Don Hennessy

To my wife Marguerite, who has helped
me understand what love is

Contents

Acknowledgements

In writing this book, I have had the good fortune to be guided, encouraged and challenged by Rio Ceederlund PhD. Rio has the extraordinary gift of making scientific sense of my thoughts. Her contribution is spread throughout the book. My hope is that she will continue to research the work and eventually produce evidence of the best way to protect target-women. I am privileged and grateful to have worked with her.

My gratitude also goes to Carmel O'Neill from Australia, who has help me explore the issue in a more in-depth way and has shared her extensive knowledge with me. Thanks to many of my current and recent clients who are aware of this book, and to tell them that I am in awe of their encouragement and their clarity. As before, I want to especially acknowledge my colleague Fionnula Sheehan, who corrected my script and supported my efforts with a powerful mixture of wisdom and energy. Any remaining mistakes are mine not hers. Finally, thanks to Sean O'Keeffe and his colleagues at Liberties Press for publishing the book.

Don Hennessy
February 2018

Part 1

Introduction

This book is written in the hope that a woman who is being abused by her intimate partner will find some help in escaping from the mental torture that underpins this abuse. It may also be of help to those men who suffer similar abuse, though I have little experience of working with such men.

The core of the message in this book is that you, the abused woman, have been mentally coerced in a way that invades your slow or analytical thinking and quietens your instinctive thinking. I hope to show you how this invasion took place without you knowing it, and how to recover your mind. Having worked with abused women for more than twenty years, I have developed a series of steps which can help to repel this invasion and help you recover the use of your intuition. This recovery will allow you to begin to think without confusion and to follow your own instincts.

This book also comes with a safety warning. My clients respond to my guidance in many different ways. Some reject my suggestions because they see some danger which I cannot assess. Some reject me because I am a man. Some begin the journey with me, only to become anxious and stuck, and do not make progress. Some walk all the way with me but are seduced back into the old relationship. Some women come back to me after several years, to see if we can work together towards making them safe. Please remember, as you read on, that you are the expert in your own safety. A book like this can be very dangerous, because I have never met your abuser, and he may have some traits which are outside the norm. If your abuser is an addict, he may have a very different persona at times. If your abuser has a mental illness, there may be times when he loses his ability to think. Though he may have one of these problems, he may retain enough rationality to continue to blame you for his behaviour. You may feel that it is your duty to care for such a man. Reading this book may help you to divest yourself of this responsibility. When you no longer see yourself as the source of his bad behaviour, you can respond to him without anger or guilt. You may still feel afraid, and even sometimes terrified: these are instinctive reactions to the risks you face. I hope that, together, we can expand your instinctive reactions so that you may begin to follow them in all parts of your life.

It almost seems as if we humans, despite the ability in the majority of us to have compassion for others, have a mental shield to protect us from fully grasping the extent of fear and pain another person experiences. It seems similar to the way we forget the full extent of pain from the time we broke a leg, gave birth to a child, ran an exhausting race, or endured some other very painful situation. We simply do not remember all the gruesome details. Perhaps this is the case when your friends and others listen to your story. We simply do not grasp the full extent of the terror. I have learned that a full understanding of the actual emotions is not necessary in order to fully trust and support a target-person. If the highly distinguishing patterns of abuse dynamics are present, I know what they imply. I hope that any reader of this book – target or other – will gain a greater understanding of their situation, despite this protective shield we humans seem to have.

It is very likely that your mind provides you with many explanations for why you get these bad feelings. These explanations are skewed by the abuser, and your situation. Do not rush to challenge the very thoughts you have: they will be virtually impossible to challenge at first. Give it time and, step by step, your reading will give you solid access to alternative thoughts. Take note of any gut feeling or fleeting thought that something bad is lurking. You will become aware that in each situation, you will get a new chance to act wisely, based on your gut feeling. Crucially, it is never too late.

Chapter One

A new way to approach abuse

I would like to invite you into my office and allow me to address my thoughts directly to you.

The path to psychological freedom from abuse goes through phases. This process is very much one of 'two steps forward, one step back', and sometimes even 'one step forward, two steps back'. The phases seem to follow each other in a roughly orderly fashion.

First, you learn about the common characteristics of the abusive behaviours. The underlying dynamics appear universal, and are repeated with almost mechanical precision, regardless of the various characteristics of the couple. You will recognise most or all the ways your partner acts, but you will learn more in depth, exactly how the abuse is so effective. You will then learn more about your reactions to this abuse: what you think, what you feel, what you do in response to these thoughts and feelings, and how you handle the abuse. Again, you will recognise most or all of the ways, but you will get a brand new framework of knowledge to understand your reactions.

At last, you will practise the new things you have learned, confirm your own wisdom and learn to take one small step at a time. The basics are easy to explain in theory, but you will have to try, and retry, several times so that you can use your learning for your benefit. Some clients do not meet the abuser physically but the person still haunts their minds. You will see that the same process of change takes place with your reoccurring thoughts about your abuser and the emotions you then feel.

Alongside this process, which will happen in your own mind, you will also find that you may start to reach out to the outside world in a new way. I know that the very thought of reaching out to family, friends or other people can make you feel helpless and numb. Don't worry about that now. Instead, be certain that I will address these feelings of hopelessness and alienation in a way that is aimed at building hope through developing solid knowledge. The hopelessness is a core feature of the abuse, and I will discuss it thoroughly. To give you a glimpse of what's coming up: I will not tell you in what ways you will make the practical changes in your life, because any such suggestions risk clashing with your personal situation, resources and desires. To use a metaphor: I cannot give each of you a detailed map of your life and relationship because I am not there to see it, and I can never understand exactly where you are, or where you want to go. Instead, I will offer you a way to draw your very own map, and I will give you several examples of how that can be done.

It may be that you have tried to change the way you handle the situation so many times, that you don't want more advice, or another way to change, because you think it won't work anyway. You've picked up this book, so perhaps you don't feel as hopeless this very moment; but at some stage while considering your situation, you might have felt confused. Let me then give you an instant example of how this map-making will happen. You'll get new knowledge, and thus find ways to walk through your situation at your own pace, and with the resources that are available to you. Here is a fact about abuse dynamics that you may have learned, repeatedly: the constant struggle to either understand the abuser, or to change the abuser or yourself to avoid further abuse (or both) has not worked. The ongoing monologue in your head, or with your friends, or with other people, such as a counsellor or social worker, is exhausting, and too often leads nowhere. This is the case for every person who is a target of intimate abuse. When you heard about learning yet another way to change yourself, it's likely that at some point you got hopeless thoughts, felt sad and angry, and put the book away temporarily. I believe that the very core of this exhaustion and hopelessness is that our everyday language lacks words to properly understand and explain coercive-controlling behaviour; this means that you have no possible way of either understanding it properly or explaining it to others. You may have sat through hours of counselling or friendly advice from others, biting back the feelings of hopelessness or anger, or even desperation, caused by not being able to make yourself understood. Neither can you understand, or explain, your abuser. You may have asked yourself how anyone can take charge over, and change, a situation that they are unable to explain.

What I try to do in this book is to approach your situation in a way that helps you find new paths through your situation, at your own pace and with the resources that are available to you. You probably know that any attempts that you have made to change either yourself or your abuser have failed to lessen the abuse. Your conversations with yourself, or with people around you, have proved futile and very tiring. I will try to guide you with a clear and simple narrative, and without the jargon or myths that surround this issue.

The very first new fact to put on your map is one that will run throughout this book. The reason why you can't make yourself understood is the very one that my client gave me. She told me: 'I'm so sick and tired of not being able to sort my head out, and not being able to think like a normal bloody human.' This is exactly what's going on. What you are subjected to is not comprehensible by usual human standards. What you are subjected to is only comprehensible if we remove some of the logic that humans use to understand each other. This may sound even more incomprehensible to you, and perhaps even provocative, but if you let me guide you into this realm of incomprehensible logic, then it will be easier to understand what's going on in your mind, and, in that way, you will be on your way to sorting your head out. You may find some benefit in reading this book: it may raise questions for you, and possibly provide some answers, even if the suggested ideas do not appeal to you. Each of my readers is invited to modify or reject these directions. I would be alarmed if what I write strikes you as just another form of control. It would be wrong that you would take my word, in opposition to your own instincts.

As it is important for your safety, I strongly urge you to act and behave in each moment in the way that feels safest to you. Do not act in ways that you think I would want or expect you to. I am well aware of the danger you are in, either psychologically or physically (or both). You've learned to cope with that danger for an extended time now, and I know that you are the expert on your everyday survival. I am aware that you sometimes need (and want) to do things that throw you right back into the abuse. This won't surprise me; in fact, I will expect just this seemingly irrational behaviour, and it won't be a reason for any criticism or blame. Quite the contrary: this very behaviour, so common to persons in coercive-controlling relationships, is one I will discuss and explain thoroughly in this book. Your safety is paramount. You know what will keep you safe. Don't drop that skill, as it is a basic part of your humanity, and it will be invaluable in protecting you for the rest of your life.

One question you might have heard several times from those who want to help you, is: what do *you* want? It is a common question because all your talking about the abuser reveals that you have little time and clarity to think about yourself. And perhaps you might have heard the same answer from yourself several times – that you don't know. You may know what you don't want, but what do you actually want? For now, take this other piece of abuse-dynamic fact with you as you keep reading. This confusion from being unable to properly identify and express what you want, but also being unable to think ahead and plan how to get it, is yet another effect of the coercive control you've been subjected to. It's an effect of constantly living in fear of being blamed and punished. As hopeless as it may sound, this very realisation, and how it affects your life and mind in various practical ways, is one of the keys to freedom. You live your own life, and deserve to plan for your future in whatever way suits you. As you regain the ability to think clearly without confusion, and with less fear, your gut feeling will start to inform your decisions. Your decisions will be based on options, and clarity, to which you do not have access at this point. But as you get there, I am confident that your decisions will be good for you, and that you will be able to cope confidently with the outcomes of your own choices.

As with all my clients, I will try to be available to you via email, and respond to any questions you may have as you read the book. I can be reached at *ndvia@ eircom.net*; your feedback is greatly appreciated.

Chapter Two

The dynamics of intimate partner abuse

Let us stay with the issue of control for a while. What makes us humans feel good in life? Is it to live in uncertainty, or to feel relatively secure about our situation? It may sound like a silly question, but consider it for a moment. How do you make sure that you stay away from confusion? Does it help you to try to analyse the source of your uncertainty, or is it the act of analysing that is the very core of your distress? Do things feel hopeless because you may not even know exactly what it is that makes you feel so distressed, or you do understand why you feel distressed, but feel clueless about how to change it? What do you do to reduce your sense of distress? My guess, based on what I hear from my clients, is that you search for answers in your partner, or in yourself. In fact, part of the distress you feel is probably the very sense of not being able to grasp the whole picture. The same thoughts come back again and again, but they lead you nowhere, and all you get is an increasing sense of pressure and desperation, frustration, shame, or simply numbness. This very inability to make sense of what you see before you, the inability to grasp the whole picture from where you are, and the feeling of hopelessness when you look for answers, is exactly what lack of control means.

Normally, when we need to relieve ourselves of unease or simply work towards something we would enjoy in life, how do we do it? We communicate. We reason with ourselves, and others. We check our inner library to see what we know and don't know already, and then we go to someone else to find out more. We ask them if they can help us; from what we learn, we make the plans that are needed; and then, off we go. As simplistic as it may seem, this is what you are doing when you try to figure out how to change the abuse, and this is exactly what your coercive controlling partner is also doing. But as an effect of the abuse, your skills to reason and communicate effectively are diminished. This lessening of your skills will cause you to jump to conclusions in an attempt to explain your fear or shame. These conclusions are like darkened alleyways that lead you into more anxiety and confusion, or may lead you to explanations that keep you in the relationship even though you wish to leave it.

It might be helpful to you if I refer to a name that I have introduced, to try and accurately indicate the kind of man who can establish and maintain an intimate relationship without taking the femininity of his partner into account. By means of a process of targeting, setting-up and grooming, the abuser achieves this goal of seducing an adult person into a relationship that is imbalanced from the start, and by re-grooming, using coercion and seduction, maintains the relationship for a long time. The sense of entitlement shines through in the arrogance of their belief that they have the right to control your thinking. The mind-control that feels like an invasion of the thinking part of your mind, and the feeling that your own voice and intuition have been drowned out, are the results of your partner's constant work to gain access to your thoughts. This relationship dynamic with an intimate abuser is dangerous, and many clients experience a sense of malevolence or evil from the person. The goal of invading your mind – to have easy access to your thoughts – which starts with a sense of being 'befriended' by the new partner, has led me to discuss the abuser in terms of 'psychephilia' and 'psychephile', terms that I introduced in my previous book. This term is used in a descriptive sense, in order to emphasise the fact that it is by the initial 'befriending' of your mind that the abuser has gained control over your thoughts (Hennessy, 2012).

The intimate abuser ignores your preferences and dismisses your opinions. As presented above, you become the focus of an intense form of mind-control, which you are unable to identify. If we caregivers and helpers can recognise and accept the power of this destructive and persistent coercion, built on a foundation of self-justification, it will focus our attention on the abuser, and acknowledge that the abused partner has no active role to play in the abuse. The community will then resist the practice of blaming the victim, and locate the problem firmly with the abuser.

I call the partner of a skilled abuser a target-person, because they are not the problem, but the focus of the abuser's problem. Being a target is a most destructive experience for any decent human (Hennessy, 2012).

The abuser

Once you start reading and learning about intimate abuse, you will inevitably come across the terms 'psychopath', 'sociopath', 'narcissist' and perhaps 'borderline'. All these terms are variations of the same thing: a label that describes a set of characteristics of people. The characteristics often include callousness and selfishness. It is not uncommon that someone, layman as well as professional, will tell you their opinion about whether or not all abusers are psychopaths. While this discussion goes on, the core issue is overlooked: the behaviour of the abuser, and the effects of this behaviour on other people. Some day, the research community might end up with a term that covers all the behaviours of an intimate abuser, but until then, I have decided to refrain from any naming in this book. Instead, I want to move to what is most essential: that the coercive controlling, deviant behaviour of the intimate abuser is identified.

Initial steps into an abusive relationship

This is a brief look at the deliberate tactics employed by every male intimate abuser in our culture. Clients who were abused by women describe the tactics as similar. In other cultures, the community may already have initiated these steps before the woman meets her abuser. In this section, I will speak as if the abuser is a man, and the target a woman. (For a more comprehensive examination of these covert tactics, see Hennessy, 2012.)

Targeting

When an intimate abuser meets a target-woman, he comes with a sense of entitlement to a relationship where he has complete sexual priority over his partner. He will seek a partner with the following personality traits:

Kindness	The woman must demonstrate that she is ready to put the needs of others before herself.
Loyalty	The woman must convince him that she will keep the secrets of their intimacy.
Dedication	The target-woman must display an ability to concentrate on her tasks and to show an energy and commitment to living up to her promises.
Truthfulness	He will demand the truth from her at all times.

A skilled intimate abuser can make an instinctive assessment of these qualities within the first few weeks of their encounter, and will persist in the relationship if he can use these qualities to move to stages two and three of the process.

Setting-up

The setting-up phase of the process runs concurrently with the third phase (grooming), but it is finite in that it will be completed when the terms and conditions of the relationship are established. The speed with which this phase is completed can vary between different cultures and religions, but the final outcome is the same for every woman.

Responsibility	The woman is given responsibility for the emotional temperature of the relationship.
Blame	She is forced to take the blame, even when she is not responsible for a particular problem.
Language	She is directed to use his language when describing their relationship.
Truth	He redefines her truth and makes it his truth.
Memory	He retells the story of their relationship in ways that enhance his position.
Esteem	He demeans her talents and exaggerates her faults.
Sanctions	He demonstrates the type and intensity of his sanctions.

Once the terms and conditions of the relationship are established, he will vigorously monitor their practice, and make sure they are adhered to. These terms are eventually embedded in the woman's thoughts, and come to overwhelm her own instinctive view of the world.

Grooming

Being liked	The target-woman will tell him what she likes and dislikes in a partner, and he will pretend to be that person.
Being understood	He will convince her that her distress is compounded by the fact that she doesn't understand him.
Being believed	He will want her to accept that what he says is right.
Being pitied	He will present his story in a way that will invite her sympathy.

Being excused	He will develop a list of excuses which he knows she will accept.
Being blameless	He will locate the blame for his abuse outside himself.
Being contrite	He will be contrite in order to avoid sanctions.
Being feared	He will increase his sanctions in direct proportion to the resistance he encounters.

This grooming process is constant throughout the length of the relationship, and is fuelled by the information he gleans from the intimate context in which the relationship is set.

The combined processes of targeting, setting-up and grooming mirror the recognised tactics of paedophiles. The tactics of the adult intimate abuser are subtler and more hidden than those of the paedophile, but they are used for similar reasons. They are subtler because they are designed to establish and maintain a long-term intimate relationship, while paedophiles seldom stay with the one target. They are more hidden because the target, being an adult, might notice them if they were overt, and because the abuser also wants us to tolerate his behaviour if he is ever challenged. For these reasons, I find the use of the word 'psychephile' both accurate and enlightening. Some of my clients find this comparison to be upsetting, and reject the idea that their intimate partner is more odious than a paedophile. I am not sure if a male intimate abuser should be judged in that way, but as I learn more about male intimate abusers, I am in awe of their skills in having us tolerate and excuse their destructive behaviour. I am also stunned by the kindness of their partners, who almost invariably do not want them to be condemned.

Having worked at a national level to try to develop an effective response to male intimate abusers, I find that the ability of the community to dismiss his destructiveness and to blame his victim echoes our response to child abuse until the last fifty years. It is time to take a serious look at what is really going on in your home, and in the homes of many other women throughout the world.

Chapter Three

The abuser: the person you meet

If the initial tactics of targeting, setting-up and grooming are covert and successful, the victim is unable to analyse her experience in terms of his behaviour. Instead, she is drawn into a lifetime of self-analysis and self-criticism, which she will present as the core problem. I want to emphasise this to any reader who meets women in their work-practice, be it as a counsellor, therapist, human-resources manager, or other professional. An employee or a client you meet who constantly returns to analysing themselves or their partner, or both, and keeps trying to understand what is wrong, might be a target of coercive control. The very act of mulling over relationship issues can become so endemic that it interferes with work, social relations or therapy, and might make a counsellor or therapist think in terms of a personality disorder. In such a case, keep coercive-controlling relationship abuse in mind. This description of the issue, as one of self-criticism and endless circles of asking why they aren't able to be better partners, is supported by the abuser, so that the couple present their difficulties as a systemic issue, one that is caused by their inability to relate to each other, or more often as a problem of inadequacy in one of the partners, most often the woman. In other words, we are invited by both parties to minimise or ignore his behaviour, and to complicate our diagnosis by means of several irrelevancies. These irrelevancies become a smokescreen by which he avoids being seen and held accountable. Our first engagement needs to lift the smokescreen and describe what is underneath. To those who work with couples, in relationship counselling or in the setting of social work, I need to stress that men can also be targets of coercive controlling abuse.

The goal of the intimate abuser is the long-term intimate control of the spirit of the target-person. He wants his demands to be met. The context of the relationship is special in that the daily routine allows him access to the innermost dreams and fears of the woman, which is the prerequisite for his acting on the sense of entitlement he is convinced is the norm. Because of this extremely narrow-minded view of the world, one that he is unable to change, he is constantly vigilant with regard to any issues regarding relationships, and especially the one with his intimate partner. Should he be told that it is his own deceitful and demeaning behaviour that causes desperation in his partner, the subsequent denial of intent to harm is based on a sense that he was right in everything he did. This is the reason he seems incomprehensible to the listener who has seen proof of his abuse. If he wants to avoid sanction, he can lie effortlessly. Most listeners hear what he says and trusts him, meaning that the blame falls on the woman, sometimes despite vast evidence of his abuse.

This astounding fact, how someone can go free from blame in the face of overwhelming evidence of the opposite, experienced by so many women who were targets of abuse, is yet another consequence of the completely different perspective the coercive controlling person has on the world. The conviction you hear from them, that they had the right to do what they did, or never intended to cause what they are accused of, is based on a lack of empathy, and a self-serving view of their world. This perspective is so fundamental that whatever the abusive man says is delivered with such complete conviction that a listener cannot get around it either. You have probably experienced this in the abusive situations many times. You have been baffled, or numbed, or confused by the sheer conviction in your partner's messages. You cannot put your finger on what it is, and you sense that something is deeply wrong, but still you cannot get around the fact that your partner is genuinely, solidly, completely convinced that he is right in what he says, and has the right to feel and do whatever he wants, based on that right. You have seen others convinced by him, even in the face of so many signs of him lying. This is another main reason for your desperation or hopelessness. You have no words to express what is happening, and it is no use trying, because he will convince anyone, and you will not be believed. Not only have you heard him say it, you have seen it happening repeatedly right in front of your eyes. Why I stress the change of perspective is, once again, not for the sake of making excuses or to elicit pity, but in order to bring understanding, and possibly to effect change. My ultimate goal is to help you to unwind the mind-control that he has established over you.

As you cannot get rid of the feeling that something is wrong, and that your partner's message lacks something, your partner is well aware of your confusion, and has simply withdrawn from the conversation as though nothing had happened. The degree to which you are unable to fully accept his point of view, because you genuinely sense that something is not right, is the same degree to which he cannot understand why you do not fully accept his view. It is not a choice for you to not agree, but you are unable to overcome the gnawing feeling that he is not right. He refuses to consider that he is not right, as to do so would allow you to see some vulnerability in him. He may be scared that if you can access his vulnerable self, you may not like him, and may even exploit his weakness.

Determined

The skilled abuser can have a determination to dominate his partner, but he also needs to monitor the reaction of the target in order to maintain a relationship with you. To stay in control of what you are thinking, the intimate abuser learns your innermost secrets, which makes him uniquely equipped to instil his terror into your mind. The intensity and damage of these focused behaviours are almost unfathomable to someone who hasn't gone through it. We simply don't know of a language that adequately describes it. In most countries, he is very unlikely to be sanctioned by the community, yet he continually modifies his abuse and violence so that he will be able to maintain his control. This modification is informed by his ability to anticipate the reaction of his target, and his violence is usually tempered by his anxiety not to overstep your limits. Because he is so keen on controlling change and unforeseen incidents, he needs to devote much energy and time to being certain in his ability to dominate your thinking. He will eventually want you to see the world his way, because then you will no longer be unpredictable to him. It will also suit his goal to make you accept that his way is better than yours. He can only achieve this domination through persistence and diligence.

Once he has achieved complete control of your thinking, he becomes determined to ensure that he remains in control. Most skilled abusers who invest so much of their energy in having a partner who takes on the roles of a mother and a sexual slave in their lives, are determined to have that person stay with them. If they suspect that they are losing control, they will increase their efforts to maintain and enhance their entitlement. If they realise that they might lose complete control of the woman, or that their criminality might be exposed, their determination may then translate into actions that are designed to forcibly end the relationship or to end their partner's life. If the woman manages to start a new life without him, he can remain determined to make her life difficult, and to use her escape to gain the sympathy of another target. I have met some abusers who persist in maintaining their control, even when the relationship has been over for a long time. Their determination to be in charge, and to be accepted by their peers, is extraordinary.

The skilled abuser may abandon his target, but only when he has already transferred his energy to controlling a replacement. He may also get to a stage where his sexual desires are no longer a priority, and he may seek other ways of achieving fulfilment in his life. I have witnessed this shift in focus by some of the men I know, but because there is still no way to compensate for the narrow, self-serving perspective of the abuser, I have yet to see a skilled abuser change from being self-absorbed, arrogant and devious. Their lack of skill in seeing a wider perspective is permanent; as a result, their determination to be in charge of their own lives, and the lives of their intimate partners, is permanent as well.

Entitled

His sexual entitlement begins to develop from his experiences and fantasies during puberty. He feeds these fantasies and becomes convinced that these urges are good, and that girls and young women are there to minister to these urges. This conviction overrides any sense of conscience that he may have developed as a young boy. Young men have told me that they know women who are urgently waiting to mate with them. As this and other such thoughts grow unhindered, a boy arrives into an intimate relationship with a clear belief that sexual activity is solely for his pleasure, and that his enjoyment is all that matters. His sense of entitlement overshadows all the havoc he brings to others. Any resistance he experiences becomes your problem, and he will justify any behaviour that he may use to get you to change your mind. His life is ruled by his sense of entitlement, so that he is unable to comprehend that his partner has her own entitlements. In the bubble of his domain, he remains blinkered to the idea that you might wish him to change. Being blinkered by his own desires, he fails to notice that his partner would like a relationship of equals. He is astounded when you may eventually decide to terminate your relationship. His sense of entitlement dominates his thinking, and you, the target woman, are at great risk of being intimidated or terrorised into staying.

Skilful

The art of being a successful abuser is built on a range of skills that include alertness and adaptability. A skilled abuser needs to be able to read the mood of the community and modify his attitude and behaviour accordingly. This shift usually occurs when the abuser realises that their violence is non-productive, and not because there has been a shift in his sense of entitlement. A skilled abuser also has the ability to anticipate and control the reaction of the victim. This is a unique skill that creates a bond between the perpetrator and his target that can survive the most appalling human degradation. This bond is established in the mind of the target, and can convince you that his intimidation and violence is your fault, and that his behaviour is a legitimate response to your inadequacies. Some skilled abusers have an innate ability to control a woman from a very young age; some may need to practise and polish their skills in a number of short-term relationships; but all skilled abusers can modify and improve their skills until they are eventually able to dominate the thinking of their target.

Focused

A skilled abuser will develop the domination of an intimate partner into a life-time project. He may plan and monitor his strategy, and may adapt and modify his behaviour, but he remains intensely focused on his goal. This intense focus is what makes the target woman believe that her partner knows what she is thinking. You may have been led to believe that this focus is a sign of love, but it is in fact his way of getting what he wants, and maintaining his control. Even when the relationship breaks down, most abusers continue to infiltrate the thinking of their former partner, in the belief that they can still rule her life. After a relationship breakdown, some abusers may abandon their immediate goal and instead dedicate their energy to establishing mind-control over another woman. Having honed their skills in their previous relationships, these abusers are more adaptable, and can hoodwink their next target in a shorter timeframe. They are also quicker in identifying targets who might be more susceptible to being groomed. I do not know of any abusers who has abandoned their desire to dominate a sexual partner.

Tolerated

Every abuser flourishes in part because we, as a society, may be ambivalent about his entitlement and about the perceived victimhood that he adopts. We can be easily convinced that his behaviour has nothing to do with us, but may be the legitimate reaction to some perceived or real slight. If we cannot lay the blame directly on the victim, we may be able to connect the victim to the system that victimised the psychephile. Our ability to tolerate this persistent and destructive behaviour is founded on our sense of separateness and helplessness. In tolerating the behaviour of a skilled abuser, not only do we support his sense of victimhood, but we also add a number of other layers, such as exploring the behaviour of the victim, our affinity for the abuser, and our ambivalence about his sexual rights. Though the abuser can cause as much havoc as the paedophile or the perpetrator of non-relationship rape, we continue to succumb to his grooming, and treat him very differently from other sexual criminals. We are bombarded with reports of the sexual crimes of both the paedophile and the rapist, but we have yet to uncover the extent of marital rape. Until we lift the lid on the sordid and sad experience of the families of skilled abusers in intimate relationships, we will continue to be hoodwinked into tolerating his behaviour.

Encouraged

The skilled intimate abuser is highly unlikely to be exposed, and even less likely to be charged or convicted. This lack of accountability is the result of our constant inability to exclude the behaviour of the victim in our analyses of the abuse. It is an important observation that all intimate abusers are able to consistently divert our gaze away from their behaviour and to redirect our attention on to the victim. It is also an important observation that these men manage to have their victims accept responsibility for the abuse, and that the victims sometimes accept a false desire to be held accountable. These seemingly contradictory facts, which result in many people colluding with the abuser, are keys to developing a better understanding of the vastly different perspective of the abuser. This collusion is a manifestation of the fundamental conviction that the abuser is not to blame for his actions. What seems like a skill, a mind of steel, or a capacity for incomprehensible callousness, is not a skill. It is not an addition to the relationship skills all humans have. It is not the ability to shut off emotions, although the abusive man can control his emotions in some circumstances, to some extent. It is the manifestation of a fundamental inability or refusal to consider another person's perspective in the first place. It is my experience that because we find it beyond belief that a man can be so deliberately cruel, we are constantly trying to excuse his behaviour and promote the idea that he is somehow incapable of being decent.

Despite all of our good intentions, society has been unable to develop a clear definition of what is happening in a relationship where intimate partner violence occurs; we have also failed to accept the context and impact of the abuse. Recently, I looked at a press photograph of what appears to be a loving couple. The day before, the woman in the relationship published a horrific picture of her recent facial injuries on social media. Radio stations broadcast expressions of sympathy for the abuser, and how the exposure will have a detrimental effect on his career. The most popular national newspaper carried an explanation by the abuser, which minimised his behaviour. Other commentators rushed to condemn the woman for having exposed her assailant, or for not having left after previous assaults. I have not seen any suggestion that the man who behaves in this way to the mother of his children should be heavily sanctioned. The exposure of this man has come after a long series of heinous crimes for which he was never challenged. If he had repeatedly assaulted a stranger, he would have been jailed.

Demanding

The demands of the skilled abuser never seem to be satisfied. When any need appears in the context of his intimate relationship, it must be sated immediately. This urgency is not driven by anxiety or fear, but by his sense of entitlement and arrogance. He is not concerned about the quality of his partner's behaviour but, using criticism and intimidation, he invades her life so intensely that she spends most of her energy serving him. You could say that he knows that he wants to be in control. Most importantly, he wants fulfilment, and to get it without delay. This means that the woman spends her life on a treadmill. The abuser controls the speed of the treadmill, and she seldom gets a chance to step off the machine. After years of effort, it begins to occur to some women that the treadmill is going nowhere, and that all her energy is being wasted. But like you, she is never allowed to take a break: even if her abuser is away from home, he can still keep her on the treadmill of his demands. As you run out of energy, he will increase his demands or change his desires. I have met women in their seventies who are expected to be at their abuser's beck and call, and some who are still expected to be sexually available. The demands of the abuser increase not because he wants improvement or perfection but because gaining complete control of your life will be an achievement for him. To make sure that you comply with the terms and conditions that he has established, he needs you to feel inadequate. This feeling of inadequacy becomes a stick with which an abuser emotionally beats you. It is also a rod with which some women chastise themselves. Instead of focusing on his incessant and ever-increasing demands, you probably concentrate on your failure to respond adequately. The abuser also focuses on your failures and presents his demands as reasonable.

Persistent

Coupled with his focus and determination, the abuser can be persistent in that he is constantly directing his behaviour and his conversation towards his primary goal. Any conversation with him will be redirected to his own agenda in a way that will feel obsessive to others. This persistence is not always a negative trait, and can sometimes be helpful in limiting our conversation with him. It is impossible to have a relationship with him because there is almost nothing in his mind beyond his agenda. If you are the target of a skilled abuser, you are chosen to be in a relationship with him, and you must spend your energy trying to access the inner world of the man you want to love, since you believe that you will find that there is something decent within him that is similar to what we expect from another human. In fact, what you encounter is a resistance and a defiance that is resolute and unyielding. You are unable to hold a conversation with him that doesn't end up in frustration for you. He inevitably moves the conversation away from your interests and redirects the agenda towards his constant need to criticise you and reject your approach. The tone, and the single-mindedness, of his conversations result in you carrying a true and accurate recording of his voice and attitude in your head. His persistence invades your thinking and causes you to engage in a constant monologue with his voice.

Lack of empathy

Most, if not all, skilled abusers are either incapable of taking, or unwilling to take, their partner's well-being into consideration. This manifests itself as an inability to recognise your suffering. He inflicts abuse on you but demands that you ignore his assaults and behave as though he had done nothing bad. The intimate abuser has no problems in sharing a bed with you, even though you may be carrying the physical evidence of his abuse. His lack of empathy can also extend to his ability to put his own needs before those of your children. Many intimate abusers have attacked their partner when she was pregnant or nursing an infant. Yet they have also demanded that they be understood or forgiven by the victims of their crimes. They may apologise in the initial phase of the relationship, but their contrition is self-serving and is never designed to soothe you but rather to encourage you to avoid sanctioning him. Not only do intimate abusers fail to acknowledge the suffering of their family but they also lack empathy for themselves. An abuser is unable to take other people's perspective into account, not only in relation to others, but also in relation to himself; as a result, his perception of existence is barren and solitary. While you are living with a skilled abuser, you will gradually learn that you will never be allowed to see into his spirit. A more realistic viewpoint is that what you see is what you get, or maybe that what you thought you saw when you fell in love, you seldom get. His lack of empathy is directed as much towards himself as towards the rest of his world. His emotional life is hidden from himself, and any attempt by you to access it will be doomed, as it will be met with contrived behaviour.

Deliberately cruel

Being deliberately cruel is a common trait in the skilled abuser. He is cruel because he has a grounded conviction that his partner deserves it. There are people who have cruel thoughts but do not act on them, and there are those who accidently bring suffering on others, but abusers are recognised by their actions and not their rhetoric. It is what they do, and not what they say, that allows us to categorise cruel people by their behaviour towards others. The skilled abuser seldom attacks anyone but his intended victim. He has developed an ability to control his anger and rage so that few people witness his behaviour. He can be equally cruel by acts of omission, such as denying his wife a visit to the dentist when she is in acute pain, denying her permission to buy new clothes, as much as by criminal behaviour. He can torture the spirit of his target to the extent that she loses her sanity. He can colonise the souls of his children and use them as weapons to attack their mother. He can deflect our attention from his behaviour to her supposed inadequacy, and leave her bereft of human support. He can torture the whole family and resist any attempt to admit the damage he is doing. He can kill his partner, his children and sometimes himself without accepting that his cruelty is unwarranted.

Intimidating

We all have the ability to intimidate others. We can do so without being aware that the other is feeling intimidated by us. Some of us are described as having an intimidating presence. The skilled abuser may develop such an intimidating presence at home that his impending arrival can create anxiety and his presence can generate fear and terror. He can do all of this while working or socialising with colleagues who have no reason to be afraid of him. He can even be regarded as one of the 'good guys' in the community, and make stories about his other persona almost unbelievable. But his ability to intimidate can be curtailed if his tactics are exposed and his behaviour punished. He is an intimidating bully who wants the community to accept him. The fear that he generates at home needs to be matched by the acceptance he garners from those outside the home. He is smart and skilful in his ability to develop two personas. He is effective and enduring in his ability to achieve and maintain his dominance. He is very frightening to his victim in his ability to get her to accept responsibility for his behaviour.

Terrifying

What is most terrifying for the partner of a skilled abuser is that she is scared of being killed but cannot explain her fear. She is afraid that she is going mad, but any attempt she makes to get us to understand the mental torture she suffers fails because she does not know that she is mind-controlled. Even if she could articulate her fear, and even if she could detail the process of being mind-controlled, she will be blamed by the community for her predicament. Instead of being warned by the police, who know that she is the victim of repeated crime, her fear is dismissed, and she is encouraged to tolerate the crime. Instead of being protected by the judiciary, she is blamed for her reticence and denied safety. Even when she is brave enough to move out of the relationship, she is obliged by the courts and social services to remain accessible to her abuser, in the mistaken belief that she is responsible for the relationship between the children and their father. This complete lack of appreciation of the experience of the target woman, and the lack of an accurate assessment of the behaviour of the man, leaves the woman unheard and terrified. This terror is orchestrated by the unacknowledged mind-control of the skilled abuser, and is facilitated by our inadequate response. The response of the community is often more terrifying than the behaviour of the man. If you are in an abusive relationship and are terrified, you have every reason to feel so. You are not imagining this feeling, and you are not responsible for it.

Liar

Many skilled abusers lie, and do so purposefully and intelligently. The abuser's purpose is always to improve his position and to give credence to his statements. His intelligence is needed to help him be coherent and convincing, and also to remind him of previous statements he has made. The art of intentionally lying can be developed to such an extent that the lying skilled abuser may find it difficult ever to speak truthfully. Abusive women and men can lead double lives and lie successfully to hide habits and behaviours that they do not wish us to know about. They lie so that we may think better of them. Their purpose is self-advancement. When their self-righteousness and self-importance matches their skills, they become immune to the truth, and exist in a world where they are in charge. The pathological liar can be quickly identified by other liars, and may find it difficult to benefit from lying in certain circumstances. He may even confess to his failings if he believes that it is in his best interests to do so. He may adapt or modify his stated position under pressure, while refusing to change his attitude or behaviour. In other words, he may appear to agree with you on a certain course of action but ignore the agreement to change, and just carry on as before. Skilled abusers behave like all other liars in relation to their intimate partner, while in other parts of their lives they can be truthful and trustworthy.

Self-absorbed

In their other relationships, they can be accepted and rewarded for their honesty, but in their intimate relationship they are afraid of being found out. They know that they have conned the target woman into an unequal relationship, and that their intention must remain hidden. Protecting this agenda becomes the focus of everything they do with you. Hiding their plan from the **woman** and their children demands that they maintain their concentration and never appear to concede that they might be wrong. They ignore or dismantle any challenge to their self-importance and never allow their partners a platform from which they can challenge their position. The skilled abuser listens when you or others talk to him. He is not listening so that he can appreciate your viewpoint but is alert to any attack on his own agenda, and watches for any opportunity to redirect the conversation and gain advantage over the speaker. He will usually redirect the topic by pretending that you said something that supports his own position. He will twist a statement and persuade you that you said something different. Discussions with an intimate abuser are futile, as he skilfully modifies what is said to suit himself. Most target women will admit that they become angry with themselves for being unable to penetrate the impregnable wall of the abuser's defences. Maintaining this wall demands that the skilled abuser focuses on his own agenda at all times.

Opinionated

A skilled liar may reserve his talent for certain occasions, but most pathological liars are happy to lie about any aspect of their lives and their behaviours. They lace their conversations with exaggerations or denials that are difficult to define as blatant lies but modify reality so that the liar appears better than he really is. I have not met any talented liar who lies to make himself look worse in any situation. The skilled abuser is better than any politician because he is always right. He will promote and modify his opinions so that we cannot unravel his arguments. He can change his opinion to suit his position, and deny that he ever held the original opinion. His opinion on the state of his relationship is irresistible, his opinion on the reasons for the state of his relationship is irrefutable, and his opinion on the remedy for his relationship is non-negotiable. He will deny us the right of any worthwhile intervention because he cannot concede that he may be part of the problem. His ability to hold to his opinions is most obvious in his discussions with you. In conversations with you, he is seldom wrong, and if he is in danger of being exposed, he can produce a new opinion and persuade you that he has not changed his position. While his opinions seem to be important to him, he can change them when it suits him to do so. He learns that in his intimate relationship, his ability to win is far more useful than seeming to hold an opinion that is not valid. His only agenda is to challenge your reasoning and destroy your opinions.

Quick thinking

A bad liar – that is, one that is easy to identify – has to conjure the lie from the analytical part of his mind: we can usually observe some physical indication that this process is taking place. He can stop for breath, he can lick his lips, or he may move his fingers or shift his eyes while he assesses how big a lie he is going to tell. These symptoms can also be identified and monitored by a lie-detector machine, which can expose the untruth in his statement. But a pathological liar does not need to analyse his statements. With practice, he can instinctively say whatever he needs to say in orfer to maintain or improve his position. This skill means that these men are difficult to recognise. The pathological liar can conjure up an instant response to any statement, in the knowledge that he can justify his response with more lies if necessary. A skilled abuser is extremely quick-thinking, as he instinctively knows what his agenda is, and he is expert at identifying a response that will be to his immediate benefit. He has no concern about the long-term implications of his statement, as he will have no difficulty in modifying or denying it in the future. He lives on his instincts, like many animals, and does not waste time on analysing his behaviours or his thoughts. He has a sharp mind and he uses his fast thinking to outwit his partner and resist our suggestions. If he is challenged by psychologists or judges, he can present himself as reasonable and concerned, and can conjure up stories about you which will guarantee that the professionals will condemn you and feel sorry for him. Successful abusers are never sanctioned, and most of them are never identified by the community.

Informed

Not alone does a good liar need to be quick-thinking, but he also needs to be informed about the people who are listening to him. His audience will dictate the content and tone of his utterances, so he is alert to the opinions of the listeners and can be practical and co-operative, or helpless and pleading, depending on what he believes will be most influential. His ability to sway his audience to be on his side, and to condemn his partner, is the main reason why his behaviour remains hidden. Even when his crimes are exposed, he avoids sanction. The skilled abuser will know if the listener believes in the goodness in everyone, and will present himself as responsible and concerned. If he believes that his listener is influenced by rights and fairness, he will present himself as entitled and denied. If he is challenged, he may revert to exaggerating his power and influence. The skilled abuser will do all of the above in the context of his intimate relationship. When his behaviour or his opinion is challenged by you, he will convince you that what he is doing is the best for you and your children. He may even convince you that his abuse and violence is for your benefit, and that you will learn from it. He will work diligently at protecting his entitlement, and claim that his rights are paramount. In most long-term relationships, he has established such control that he can persuade you that any challenge to his authority will have serious consequences for you and the family. He will know you in a deep psychological way, and will use this information to manipulate your thinking. This knowledge is unique to the context of an intimate relationship: in short, he probably knows more about your inner world than any other person.

Shallow emotions

Many abusers have few if any genuine friends. They surround themselves with allies or victims. They go through their day seeking what is good for them, and use others to get what they want. Their allies are people who want the same or similar things: they co-operate in pursuit of their goals, but they move away from their allies once a particular goal has been achieved. They can be active business partners but, if successful, they can cut their partner off and try to colonise all the success. They can have many victims, whom they manipulate into acting for them, but they never reveal their ultimate goal to these people. The intimate abuser wants his target woman to be both his ally and his victim. His incapacity for love means that all his protestations of affection and dependence are false. It is his capacity to appear to be emotionally attached that keeps you in the relationship, even when you are paying a huge price for your commitment. He may try to persuade you that he would die if you ever left him, because he would be unable to survive emotionally without you. His emotions are shallow and false. A skilled abuser has feelings only for himself; many partners realise this, not in the passion of their own intimacy but in the intimate abuser's observable grooming and manipulation of their children. It is very frightening to realise that when he appears to be angry or sad, he is really only acting, and that he can switch from rage to tears in an instant.

Need for stimulation

Many abusers tend to live on the edge. They want some sort of excitement in their lives, and can take many risks, in the belief that they can get away with bad behaviour by lying about their own involvement and deliberately placing the blame on others. They frequently engage in promiscuous behaviour, gambling or alcohol abuse, but can hide their involvement, or deny it, if challenged. The intimate abuser will bring this need for stimulation into his intimate relationship and may expect to have that need fully satisfied by one person. Many abusers continue their engagement with alcohol, gambling or promiscuity, and seem to enjoy the challenge of the woman when she pleads with him to stop these behaviours. They are further stimulated by their ability to disrupt the life of the woman, and to claim that it is her nagging that drives him to be abusive and violent. Having a sexual slave can be the ultimate stimulation for some abusers. It is also emerging that the abuser may engage sexually with his children when he is no longer satisfied with the sexual service provided by their mother. A skilled abuser with these behaviours can do more damage within the family than a paedophile who invades the family. It is traumatic for children to be used as a buffer by a parent, and a child who is sexually abused by a parent has the added anguish of being betrayed by someone who should love them.

Many abusers believe that they are the focal-point of their own worlds. They see themselves as gods in their own universe, and are hugely concern about their image among their peers. This trait is probably an impetus for the increase in their dangerous behaviours if they are ever at risk of being exposed and having their behaviours revealed. It may also explain why they continue to abuse their targets long after the relationship has ended. They cannot allow their former partners to appear victorious, and they will intimidate you and speak badly about you so that others will have some sympathy for them.

Along with these attributes, these men are often extremely clever con-men, and can present themselves in ways that will encourage the listener to be groomed by them. They are chameleons who can adopt the most suitable persona in any circumstance, and can quickly vary that persona if they realise that change is needed. Added to all these characteristics is a universal sense of entitlement which allows the skilled abuser to turn his full attention to you, the target woman. You become his lifetime project; you have no idea of the combination of skills and energy that he employs to dominate your humanity, your femininity and your sexuality.

The intimate abuser brings all these talents and tactics to bear on you as his only target woman. You become the focus of his terror and lies. The profound effect of this immoral force is to establish his control over your mind and body. The violence and abuse are driven by his overarching sense of entitlement. It is his intention, which becomes his universal project, to makes your life hell and our interventions inadequate. We need to see what is going on. We need to redefine the process and to establish the activities and the goals of

27

every skilled abuser. In order to do so, we need to re-examine the definitions of intimate abuse which are currently in use, and modify them to include both the intention and the behaviour of the abuser.

Sexual control

An abuser sets out to control their partner because he or she wants to dominate all the activity in the relationship; in a partner-relationship (contrary to a friendship or a parent-child relationship), the most personal and intimate form of control is sexual. Most cultures, and many of the world's religions, have colluded with male abusers over the centuries. Under the guise of the 'survival of the species', men have been encouraged, and maybe even obliged, to procreate. This encouragement ignores the wishes of the woman: many cultures and religions support the idea that a man's sexual desires are paramount in an intimate relationship. Humans may be the only species that encourages intercourse even when the female is unwilling or unprepared. Most animal mating occurs when the female is in heat, and the sole purpose of mating is procreation. Most male mating engaged in by the male abuser ignores the female cycle, and happens when it suits the man. When I explore the sexual experiences of my clients, I find that very few of them have any sort of sexual autonomy in the relationship. You may recognise that you, like many of these women, are a second-class citizen in the marriage bed, and comply with the sexual demands of the male out of fear, or out of a recognition that not doing so would confirm his belief that you are sexually inadequate. You may also be under pressure to try and convince him that you are not having an affair; any unwillingness on your part to have sex with him may be interpreted by him as proof of your betrayal.

The idea that a man has to abuse his wife to gain control or status within the family ignores the reality that man has always had the power and status within the family. When the abuser enters into an intimate relationship, he wants to have access to all kinds of gratification, including sexual gratification, when he wants it. Or, in the case of abusers who are not interested in sex, they want the benefits of, and the control they get from, an intimate relationship without having to deal with the sex. Through the process of mind-control, and by proclamations of love and affection, these abusers can live this self-focused life, where their agenda is to get what they want. They adopt a loving persona until they have set up their target. Once they have achieved control, the loving persona disappears. Many target women spend their energy trying to access the reasonable man that seduced them in the first place. You may even get an occasional glimpse of the attractive man who seduced you, and this glimpse will keep your hope alive that he can be decent and respectful.

Some abusers may be sexually demanding, while others may wish to hide their sexual inadequacies, their sexual deviance, or their sheer lack of interest in sex. The effect of being rejected by a partner who wants to hide his true sexuality can be more damaging for a woman than the effect of being subjected to incessant demands. Deep pain is experienced by a loving woman who is rejected by the man who promised to love her. Being told that she is no longer attractive, or that she is sexually inadequate, can be devastating for any woman. Either way, the abuser will be in charge of the level of sexual activity between them, and will dictate the practices and frequency of all sexual encounters. The target partner is condemned to a secondary role, and is not allowed to negotiate her wishes.

The male abuser arrives into the relationship with a strong belief that he is sexually designed to be the boss, and will not concede sexual equality to you.

Kate and Ciarán were a very sociable couple in a small town. Kate was from a working-class background and Ciarán was from a wealthy family. They had a large circle of friends and he had a number of siblings who lived locally. Kate felt she had done well to be in relationship with such a prominent family, especially as she already had a child before she met Ciarán. She felt that the child would have a much better upbringing and have greater opportunities for a good education if she married him. Before she was married, she hid her anxieties, even from herself, and ignored her gut feeling that there were aspects of Ciarán's behaviour that she did not like.

On her wedding night, she went to bed on her own and woke to find her husband still in his wedding attire, lying on top of the bed and very drunk. This was the start of what she calls her nightmare. She could not explain that her idea of marriage included a life of intimacy that would allow them to be affectionate occasionally without him being drunk. Years later, she realised that all their sexual encounters, both before and after marriage, involved copious amounts of alcohol.

She had two children with Ciarán but was always conscious that her sexual experiences were unfulfilling. Any attempt to negotiate a pleasurable sexual encounter was dismissed as her lack of understanding and technique. Kate was also repeatedly told that her body was damaged because she had a child outside of wedlock, and because she had lost her youthful figure and was now an 'old cow' who was incapable of enjoying anything. When she resisted taking the blame for her unhappiness, she was beaten and silenced.

Kate continues to live with her abuser. She knows she is still at risk of assault. She is scared that Ciarán will find out that she has evidence that he is having an affair with a young man who works with him. He may accuse her of being devious, or he may force her to reveal the source of her information. This information has helped her to make sense of the last twelve years of her life. She no longer challenges Ciarán and has put a plan in place to be free of him in two more years.

The prospect of being free of the charade that is her marriage keeps Kate from giving up hope, but she is very anxious about the effects of the breakdown on her children. She struggles with how she is going to explain her decision when the time comes for her to leave. She is very reluctant to reveal the truth about Ciarán to the children. She doesn't want to betray his secret to them, but she also wants to avoid being blamed for her decision. She has frequently been told by Ciarán that she cannot leave, as he would tell the children that she was mad. He has also threatened that he will pursue full custody of the children and limit her access to them.

This struggle for Kate lies between her desire to be loyal and kind to her partner while knowing that she will suffer as a result of being blamed for the ending of the relationship. My plea to Kate is to give some kindness and loyalty to herself and to demand that Ciarán be honest with her children, and at least admit that he is partly responsible for the breakdown in their relationship. I suggested to her that her husband has been living a lie and that she can offer him an opportunity to change. This may be the only chance that Ciarán has to avoid an old age spent in isolation. Kate is aware that giving her kindness to people who do not appreciate it is draining her energy and reducing the emotional clarity that she needs in order to be a good parent. Not all skilled abusers are sexually the same, but all of them blame their partners if their sexuality is challenged.

The successful repetition of his sexual demands (or the successful avoiding thereof) means that the abuser learns what he needs to do to get his own way. He will test the limits of this control as the relationship develops, and monitor his ability to achieve his sexual desires (or avoid sex) without too much effort. He will practise and hone his skills until he is certain that he is in charge of the sexual activities in the relationship.

Like most target women in a heterosexual abusive relationship, you may be ambivalent about your sexual autonomy and may believe that, having been intimate, you have lost the right to abstain if you do not wish to have sex.

The abuser will downgrade your sexual prowess until you feel that you are a slave to the abuser's sexual pleasure. If you are ever tempted to refuse his advances, you know that the pressure will intensify until you eventually concede. The recognition of the abuser's ever-increasing power to dominate your sexual response, coupled with a growing sense of effortlessness on their part, gives them a godlike feeling of certainty and freedom. The certainty is founded on the awareness that they have a range of tactics that have been proven to be effective. The freedom is based on the realisation that he will achieve his goals via various means, without suffering any sanction for bad behaviour.

If the abuser is sexually inadequate or is bisexual or gay, he may not want his target to reveal this secret. Instead, he will blame the lack of intimacy on the target's attitudes or demands, and convince the target that he is sexually competent, and that the target's difficulties are a result of her lack of experience or frigidity, or because of emotional or psychological damage suffered in her previous sexual relationships. If you are in a relationship with this type of abuser, you are not alone: I am encountering such relationships more and more as time goes by.

Either way, you will begin to focus on your own performance and become ashamed that the level of intimacy in the relationship is poor. The abuser relies on this shame to protect his deviousness, and seldom misses an opportunity to reinforce it. The abuser will compound the target partner's shame if they have any knowledge of their partner's previous sexual activity. Any such information becomes a powerful weapon in the abuser's ability to torture the target's spirit. The abuser will offer no sympathy, and may even condemn and punish their partner for their actions. If you have had an unhappy sexual experience in the past, your partner will punish you by referring to it as an explanation for your lack of intimacy.

The successful intimate abuser relishes this sexual power and feeds on his ability to exercise it. They become immune to the difficulties created for their partner, and can vary or intensify their sexual demands at will. The pleasure they experience from being sexually dominant enhances their entitlement and adds fuel to their persistence. They see themselves as the lords and masters of their partner's sexual life, and gradually objectify their partner: the abuser changes his partner's position from one of being a human companion to one of being a sexual object. When the partner resists, or struggles with, this objectification, the abuser becomes aggressive or seductive, until the partner reverts to acting out the script which has been written for her.

Jim and Betty met when she was twenty-one and he was twenty-eight. She had just graduated from college and he was working in a recruitment agency. He had interviewed her, and afterwards he had asked her for a date. They met about a week later. After he had gone with him to see his upscale apartment, she was raped by him. When she recalls that night, she still believes that what happened was not rape. She believes, because he told her, that all the women he had dated knew that they were going to have sex on the first night. He persuaded her that her problem was her lack of experience, and that she should accept that what happened was 'no big deal'.

Betty continued to see Jim, as she was convinced that she would eventually get rid of her inhibitions and learn to accept his love for her. She became pregnant and moved in to live with him. He ignored any requests she made for intimacy or even affection, but would demand sex acts that she found abhorrent. He refused to attend any pre-natal classes but came to the birth claiming that he wanted to record the dramatic event on his phone. He was so demanding in the labour ward that he was ejected by the security staff. Betty was horrified, but excused his behaviour by telling me that he was very nervous. She also explained the fact that she was raped on her first night back home after the baby was born as an expression of his desire for her.

Because of her health, Betty was advised to avoid getting pregnant for a year, but Jim insisted that she was not to take any precautions, because his child needed a sibling. They had three children in four years, even though Betty was becoming increasingly anxious about her health. Within a few months of her last birth, Betty was hospitalised with a kidney problem. It later emerged that she had been punched hard on her back and that he had known for years that the medics had been worried that her kidneys were weak. While in hospital, she learned that her babysitter had been sexually assaulted by Jim and had left the house. Betty's sister took care of the children until Betty came home.

Betty accepted Jim's denial of the assault, and agreed to stand by him if he was to face charges. When she came to me, she asked for my help in supporting both her and her husband through this difficult time. I suggested that I meet with Jim, as I was uncertain whether I could help him. Jim spent a full session with me trying to convince me that the babysitter was a liar and that he was worried that this accusation would break up his marriage. He explained to me that he was carrying a weight of responsibility, as Betty was unhealthy and he had to organise everything in relation to the children. He was very convincing, but like all skilled abusers the story he told was about his achievements and his partner's inadequacies. He did not ask for help from me but suggested that I try to motivate Betty to be a better wife.

Betty came for a few sessions and seemed content to support Jim as best she could. It emerged that the babysitter had recorded a threatening phone call from Jim, in which he had threatened to rape her unless she withdrew the charges. Jim was never prosecuted but Betty was no longer susceptible to his grooming. She eventually moved back to her parents' home, and now has a good life with her children. Jim has a new partner and does not visit his children.

When Betty was asked what had been most helpful for her in meeting me, she surprised me by saying that the key thing was that I was a man. She would not have attended initially if she had known who I was, because she believed that all men were the same when it came to sex. She said that as she realised that Jim's behaviour was not the norm, she felt relieved. This relief allowed her to remove the burden of blame she was carrying. She says she would still be with Jim, and she would still be subjected to his criticism, if she had not been informed of his deviousness.

Chapter Four

The effects on you

This chapter sets out to make a detailed list of the effects of the constant mental cruelty that you have suffered. It will also begin to examine the impact on a person like you when you share an intimate life with a skilled abuser, and to help you recognise that, though you may be uncertain, there is a core part of your being that is not damaged. I use the term 'target-person' to help explain that your role in his behaviour is largely dictated by him, and that his focus on you is like that of a clever stalker.

In order not to lose control – which would make him very, to extremely, uneasy – he stalks your thoughts without appearing to listen to you. You may or may not notice how he tries to invade your mind. To become more aware of when he does it, and how he does it, is one of the useful details of the new map you are drawing now. This is how I suggest the way you are being constantly scrutinised can be explained. Your partner needs to scrutinise you in this way for two reasons. The first one is similar to the urge and drive many of us feel to check our social-media feeds. There is a build up inside when we do not have free access to our smartphones, laptops or other devices. When we finally get to do that scroll, a sense of well-being is released in the body, and the impetus to scroll is thus rewarded. Because we humans are used to explaining our behaviours in rather complicated ways (the blessing and curse of psychology, perhaps), neither your partner nor you will understand this behaviour from a very basic need-reward point of view. Your partner is likely to tell himself that he has valid reasons to check on you. The other reason he checks has to do with the urge to maintain control. If you have been distant from him for some reason, such as physically away, or simply preoccupied with something, he senses a change that is frustrating to him. From the basic viewpoint that others are only out to harm him by blaming or punishing, it is logical that he feels an urge to check. This does not excuse the behaviour. It does not justify violating your integrity. But it is an explanation that might help you see that there was nothing you did in the first place that put him constantly on his toes to look inside your brain. He continually yearns to search for and observe your thoughts; if he finds something threatening, he will monitor your explanations and feed his obsession until he is sure he has neutralised the threat. This process forces you to reject your own intuition, because whatever you do to act on it will be scrutinised, blamed and punished. But your instincts remain intact, even though you do not use them: with every inch you get out of harm's way, you will be an inch safer to letting your gut feeling start to guide you again.

This scrutiny, and the effects of it, are hidden from you, but you probably sense it somehow. Most importantly, it remains unspoken in your efforts to seek help. There is something unexplainable in your experience; in conversation with any helper, be they professional or friend, you may want to explain your difficulties in terms of your own inadequacies. You will want them to examine your role in the relationship as though you had some influence over it, and some autonomy within it. You will present a description of your behaviour in your partner's language, and using terms which have already been used repeatedly by him. You may want us to support you in coping with your abuse. You may also want us to feel sorry for your abuser and not to blame or condemn him.

You have been seduced, manipulated and mind-controlled from the start

What you may have been unaware of so far is that your partner has engaged in this process of seduction, manipulation and mind-control since you first met him. It will be useful for you to learn how your abuser has established his control, and how this was achieved by colonising your thoughts and invading your thinking, because this knowledge brings relief from blame and fresh eyes with which to view your situation. You may be relieved (and perhaps slightly alarmed) to learn that your instincts may have been shut down and that your ability to discern your options may no longer be accessible to you, or that your access to them is vastly limited. Your positive personality traits, your will to do good for others, and your ability to forgive, have all been tampered with to such an extent that you have lost control over them, and they are now being used against you in a subtle and persistent way which is painful, destructive, degrading and dangerous.

Because of your willingness to do what is best for others, you will easily be seduced into learning, and eventually anticipating, the needs of your abuser. You have discovered his needs quickly in the relationship, and you will have learned his likes and dislikes within a short time. His likes may not be completely revealed at the beginning, but you will be drawn into an ever-expanding scenario where his likes may become almost unbearable. You may have already told yourself that if he had revealed his complete list of likes at an early stage, you would have left the relationship. Many of my clients have told me that when they found out that the abuser's likes included behaviours that they did not condone, they found themselves attempting to modify their own behaviour to accommodate his desires. But this accommodation is a progressive process, and is gradually expanded until some of my clients become ashamed of their own behaviours. It may come as shock to you, or as a relief (or both), that the thing your partner wants is not the actual thing he pushes you to do. He is dependent on constantly keeping you surprised, and uneasy, because otherwise he would soon lose track of your mind again. Further, by coercing you to do what he wants you to do, he feels in control in a relationship – which is something he lacks in most other areas of his life, since we humans are constantly engaged in relating to others. The very sense of control he gets from coercing you is instantly stimulating to him, and the more the actions deviate from what you or society would accept, the more stimulating it is to him, simply because the bigger the deviance from normality, the greater the thrill.

His dislikes will be more apparent from the beginning. You were made aware almost immediately of the habits that you have which are unacceptable to him. As soon as you step out of line, you will have been reminded of his upset, and will be challenged to avoid upsetting him. This process of instant challenge will be swift from the beginning, and he will be diligent and alert in not letting any such behaviour pass without expressing his annoyance. If the behaviour persists, the abuser will have introduced consequences for your lack of cooperation, and will develop an incremental series of sanctions that will intimidate and frighten you. He will also demand that you accept that you are the cause of his upset, and that the cause of your suffering is your careless or inadequate behaviour.

The skill of the intimate abuser is to initiate, and to increase, these sanctions without you being aware of his tactics or his agenda. You will accept being corrected from the beginning because the offender will present his dislikes as normal. You will also accept these early corrections because you are seduced into believing that if you improve your behaviour, the relationship with him will be easier and less tense. If you tend to be a poor timekeeper, he will present himself as hating people who are late. If you tend to be a careful dresser, he will express himself as disliking vain people. If you drink alcohol, he will decry women who get drunk. If you are reluctant to be sexually intimate, he will castigate all frigid women. If you had previous sexual partners, he may tell you that you were a slut, or he may persuade you that you are sexually inadequate and that you are lucky because he will educate you sexually. If you have children from a previous relationship, or if you had an abortion, he will use that knowledge to expand your guilt. If you have already had an experience of intimate abuse, he will portray himself as your saviour. He will be able to observe the strength of his control by monitoring the speed with which you will accept his suggestions and acknowledge how reasonable he is.

You will also be groomed into taking the blame, and will examine your own behaviour and attitude. You will take the focus away from his demands, and may even be grateful for his tolerance. Like most target women, you can be persuaded that this tolerance is an expression of his love, and you can be seduced into a deeper relationship by his apparent forgiveness. He will make his instant demands and subsequent criticism in a way that encourages you to put yourself in the position of responsibility. He will gradually increase his range of dislikes so that you begin to realise that he is difficult to please; by now, you may believe that nothing will please him. Once you accept this trend, you are put on a treadmill of failure, which drains your energy. He can regulate the speed and the incline on this treadmill until you are devoting all your efforts to surviving on this machine. When you believe that you have succeeded, he will deny you any reward and remove the possibility of you pleasing him.

Like all my clients, you probably function as though nothing is wrong, and continue to meet the normal demands of everyday life. You can fulfil several roles, including housekeeper, sexual partner, mother, carer and professional without ever being given even a modicum of appreciation. It is the fact that no worthwhile appreciation is offered by the abuser that takes you to the limit of your endurance. Throughout my life, I have come to recognise the energising effect of human appreciation. It is very hard to comprehend how any woman or man could survive living with an abuser knowing that they are being deprived of the fuel of appreciation. But all my clients keep going: like you, they are convinced that they have no option. It is infuriating to me to hear professional experts claim that you have choices when you have very little ability to assemble options on which to base your choices. Your abuser has convinced you that you have no options, and he has undermined your ability to make intuitive choices. Your autonomy has been eroded to a point that you may begin to doubt your own judgement. This book is not designed to persuade you that you have options, or to encourage you to make choices that seem reasonable or healthy. Instead, I want to restore your instinctive voice and support you in making whatever decisions are attractive to you.

Once again, to further support the drawing of your new map, I want to use the shift in perspective to discuss this lack of support. I am sure that others have asked you, or you have asked yourself, how it is possible that you can accept living with someone who never gives you credit. From a common-sense point of view, it could easily be seen as incomprehensible that you put up with someone who willingly holds back praise just to torture you. But to get a wider picture, let me open the door to the mirror-image world. In this world, the world of the abuser, no one but himself can ever be considered when it comes to any action. He has the right to everything you do for him; thus, he does not need to thank you. This looks like arrogance, and it is indeed an arrogant behaviour, but to fully grasp the profound quality of this conviction, you must leave any common sense behind.

In any action where your partner has the time to think, he is consciously acting in the way that suits him best, and he is aware and proud of that ability because he can sense that most people do not behave like that. To him, this caution is the same as cowardice. Most coercive-controlling men sense, somehow, that it is not cowardice but true control and wisdom, something they profoundly lack. This belief only makes them double their arrogance and grandiosity, so that they can diminish any sense of inferiority. But this profound and instant self-righteousness also means that it takes effort to acknowledge anything that has nothing to do with them. Yes, it's true, you might not believe this, but do give the thought a try. It is possible for this man, of average intelligence or even higher, to watch his woman, with all her strengths and capabilities, and still have serious problems grasping in what way he should praise her or encourage her. Even if he wanted to use positive reward to make you keep doing things that are indirectly good for him, such as getting a better education or applying for a new, better-paid job, he is unable to grasp the ways in which this would benefit him.

The inability to see other points of view includes an inability to consider in what way any benign action that is not directly affecting him could be of benefit to him. His detection system is directed to identify blame or threat to him. If you do something that does not immediately affect him in a positive way, it means to him that you are doing something that either directly or later will deprive him of what is rightfully his. So, not only is it very hard for him to even detect and name what it is that he should praise, even if he can see things that could be praised (because you tell him, or he can logically grasp it), his sense of superiority would get in the way, and he would feel slighted by your success. So he keeps back praise to punish you for making him feel slighted. It is beyond his abilities to get an instant hunch to be thankful. Should he be consciously reminded that a thank-you is the correct response, by his own thoughts or by you, he will feel instantly blamed for his oblivious behaviour, which would cause him to feel hurt and in need of punishing you, until he felt that respect and justice had been restored.

Another aspect of the behaviour of a skilled abuser that seems almost unbelievable is the tactic of using public displays of false appreciation, which further erodes your self-esteem. These public displays can range from giving you cars or holidays, or flowers or jewellery. These gifts are seldom what the woman wants, but are dictated by the effect they will have on the image of the abuser, and by the manipulation that the woman knows is the real core of his message. If you have been the subject of these acts of deliberate embarrassment, you may feel completely helpless in the face of his self-serving generosity, and will quickly learn that any inappropriate response will be described as ungrateful and vindictive. All kind women would be abhorred to hear themselves described in such terms, and he knows that you will learn to swallow your pride and allow him to enhance his reputation.

As you walk further onto the playing field designed by your abuser, you may begin to realise that you are playing his game. You will learn that he writes and rewrites the rules. You will discover that the abuser in your life is the referee and sole adjudicator of the value of any move. Like most players, you will discover that challenging the referee can lead to sanctions. You will become acutely aware that he can move the goalposts both sideways and further away. Whatever ball is in play belongs to him, and he can take it away and introduce another one whenever he wants. He can also withdraw from the game when it suits him, and leave you hurt and abused on the pitch. Sadly, he can do all of this knowing that he may never be challenged or sanctioned.

Many target women develop a never-ending monologue in their heads, which becomes a living entity in their minds. Like them, you may spend time in your imagination as you discuss your survival repeatedly with him, and listen to his objections to your opinions and his criticism of your behaviours. This conversation goes on throughout the day: like many abused women, you may continue to carry on this monologue while you are asleep. You may experience nightmares about the hopelessness of your life and the helplessness of your best efforts to resolve the difficulties in your intimate relationship. This one-sided conversation is energy-sapping, as there is never a satisfactory conclusion. It is also extremely distracting and can influence your ability to do your chores in the home and to do an efficient job outside of the home; most upsettingly, it can become an insurmountable barrier between you and your children.

A self-absorbed and anxious parent puts the parent-child relationship at risk, and leaves the children troubled by the parent's distress. The parent's distress is also exacerbated by the realisation that they cannot hide their children from the devious person who is, most often, their father, but sometimes their mother. Knowing that the devious parent can play games with their young minds generates a fear, which is impossible to manage. Many of our clients have suffered extraordinary abuse while trying to defend their children from the intimidation inflicted on them by their father. This abuse is exacerbated if the child in question is not the natural child of the man.

When I, as the professional who works in this area, meet you, I must keep these experiences in mind. I need to acknowledge the effects that these experiences would have on any human being, and resist judging you on my terms, until I have established the extent of the mind-control to which you have been subjected. Many professional helpers, be they counsellors, psychotherapists or psychologists, will want to diagnose the problem in terms of your own inadequacies. This diagnosis will be encouraged by your self-analysis, and your conviction that most of the problem is your fault. This diagnosis ignores the skill, motivation and intention of every skilled abuser, and sets you up for further degradation.

You may be unable to think

Our minds seem to be divided into two main areas of thinking. There is the instant, quick-thinking function, where many of us make the majority of our decisions, and there is the slow and reflective part of our mind, where we examine the issues and find reasons for our responses. The skill of the male intimate abuser is honed on his ability to split these two functions in the mind of any woman he wishes to seduce. Once he can split the instinctive and the reflective minds, he will invade the reflective function and fill it with his own rationale.

This split is not difficult to achieve, but his skill is in doing it without being noticed, and while the woman believes she is still capable of reflection. This method is like hypnotism without the cooperation of the subject. It demands a superior level of skill, as indicated by a conversation I heard in a garage workshop one day.

A famous throat surgeon had a minor problem with his car. Being a very inquisitive and difficult man, he stood looking over the shoulder of the mechanic while the young man tried to identify the cause of the problem. As every tradesman knows, there is nothing more discombobulating than an inquisitive customer who wants to know what the issue is before you know it yourself. In the hope of encouraging the surgeon to move away, the mechanic said that what he was doing in extracting and replacing faulty parts was very similar to what the surgeon did in his work. 'You may think so,' said the surgeon, 'but the real skill is that I must operate while the engine is running.'

The skilled abuser operates while the engine is running, but also without any visible sign of the invasion, as they do not initially inflict physical pain, and they do not create any visible scars. There is no evidence that they are discarding your own thoughts from your mind, and certainly no trace of their deep incisions. But they invade the mind like any brain surgeon, and seem to implant their thoughts, while you are led to believe that you are benefiting from their superior knowledge. The emotional scars that they inflict remain hidden, and if they are ever challenged, the abuser will deny that they intended to cause them.

This emotional surgery is supported by your own wilful sharing of your innermost thoughts and fears with your abuser. They learn what makes you happy, sad, frightened, anxious, confused and guilty, not by being an armchair psychologist, but by encouraging you to reveal your inner world to them. When I hear my client saying that their abuser never listens, I reassure her that they do listen. What they do not do is respond in a comforting manner to your emotional life. Instead of comforting your distresses, they will experiment with ways of intensifying them. Instead of rejoicing in your happiness, they will develop ways of isolating you from the experiences that bring you joy. Every target partner knows that the abuser can pull a range of triggers, and evoke whatever response they wish to. If you have shared your life for an extended time with a skilled abuser, you will find that they strip you of your emotional shield and dictate your response by anticipating it. They may appear to be very clever in achieving this level of control, but in reality all they have done is listen, and learn the secrets of your inner world. He finds them and remembers them excellently, because they are highly stimulating to him. Once he has that degree of access to your mind, he can control your thinking and orchestrate your emotions.

What makes this book unique is that it attempts to make changes while the engine is running. This means that your abuser is active in your mind and has access to your thoughts in a way that is hidden and dangerous. All your positive hopes and dreams, and all my suggestions, can be drowned out by the persistence and volume of his condemning voice. We both need to be cautious.

The challenge for me when I meet a client such as you, is to accept in a profound way that your very thinking, expressed in the things you say and the way you reason, has been highly influenced and skewed. Sometimes, no matter how you and I might try, there is still a feeling of misunderstanding. After being coerced and controlled for a long time, you may no longer have access to your full thinking: to some extent, you have lost your emotional control. The understanding of what an intimate relationship is supposed to be might also be skewed. If your mind has been taken over by your abuser's voice, you probably measure my suggestions by his standards. The fear and hopelessness might also make my suggestions and advice sound useless or even threatening. When I try to draw a clear picture of his motivation and tactics, you may resist my interpretation of your reality, because you are unable to dismiss your own role in the relationship. Or you may want to defend your abuser and encourage me to accept the explanations and excuses that you have already accepted. You will be reluctant to allow me to denigrate him; even if you are angry, it is likely that you are angry with yourself.

I met Joan when I was starting this work with male intimate abuse. After a few sessions, I began to explain to her how her thinking had changed and how her life was being manipulated by her violent partner. I suggested to her that her sex life was being dictated by her husband, and that her efforts in bed were driven by a belief that if she was 'good in bed', the abuse and violence would stop. She thought I was mad. She stopped attending when I suggested that her husband might be unfaithful, and that her children, who did not talk to their father, may be more clear-thinking than she was.

When she had written evidence that her husband was in a long-term relationship with another woman, she came back to me. She berated herself for being a fool and for ignoring my insights. I agreed with her that I should have been subtler with her, but she acknowledged that everything I had said was rejected in her mind by the overpowering voice of her abuser. She told me that before she had the evidence, she would have accepted his lies, against any suggestion that he was being unfaithful. She also told me that her older children knew about the affair, but that they had stayed silent because they knew she would not believe them. They also knew that Joan would give their father priority and that, as children, they would be scolded for being against their father. Joan's mind was colonised in such a powerful way that neither her children nor I could attain any foothold in her thinking.

This skewed thinking, resulting from the abuse, is the foundation-stone that made it possible for him to rape and degrade her, and engage in constant disrespect of her human dignity. The mind-control and other degrading behaviours become the bars of the prison for the partners of every abuser. Joan resisted the idea of rape in her relationship, and expressed the view that she engaged in sexual activity willingly, even after serious assaults. But she began to change her view when she remembered that she had made it a condition of the relationship that she would not tolerate infidelity, and that she would never sleep with her abuser if he betrayed her. She also came to realise that the process by which he assaulted or intimidated her was the gateway to her acceding to energetic sexual encounters, in the belief that her enthusiasm would motivate him to change.

I learned a lot from working with Joan. I witnessed her selfless dedication to her children, her siblings and her ageing parents. I discovered her extraordinary business acumen and her boundless energy. I was in awe of her devotion to her violent and abusive partner, and the level of sympathy and support that she lavished on him. While she was in his control, she put him first in all her thoughts and tried to achieve the standards he set for her.

She claims that the day she demanded that he leave the house, and the relationship, was the first time she had seen clearly the kind of man she had lived with. In spite of over twenty years of listening to him saying he would die without her and the children, he moved directly into the home of his mistress without offering an apology or even saying goodbye.

Joan is now able to think clearly: her description of her former partner includes a number of swear-words. She recalls that she had met other counsellors who had encouraged her to 'improve' her behaviour. The reason why she thought I was mad was because I had told her that any improvement would make no difference to her partner and his agenda. She has repeatedly thanked me for my insights, which she says were chillingly accurate. I owe Joan much more gratitude than I can ever express, because it was she who first allowed me to discuss her experience of sexual abuse and who confirmed to me the process by which her abuser had dictated their sexual activity. She also alerted me to the power of being rejected when she made sexual advances, and to the lack of appreciation she experienced, which left her drained of energy. I know that I would never have got this education from a book.

You no longer listen to your instincts

In his best-selling book on how we make decisions, *Thinking Fast and Slow* (2011), Daniel Kahneman challenges us to recognise that most of our decisions are made in an instant, and even if we deliberate at length on the issue, we will probably go with our initial decision. The woman who is subjected to the tactics of a skilled abuser is unable to access her instinctive response to any family or relationship issue. She becomes unsure and hesitant initially, and eventually she becomes passive and withdrawn. While she is on this journey, she may sometimes take a stand about one of her own principles or in support of her own experience. If she persists in her stand, she quickly learns that she is at risk of intimidation or violence. She may go through the whole relationship without ever being assaulted, but she must concede to his opinions and actions.

You have been encouraged to hide your own instinctive response to any issue because the entire foundation of your partner's sense of security is that he can anticipate what you will say and do. Should you act on your own instincts, and not in the way he has taught you consistently to act, your response would become random to him, and trigger a great deal of anxiety and frustration on his part. Frustration costs energy, and if he is not in need of stimulation or revenge, then becoming angry or worked up is destructive. This is why expressing your opinions will put you at risk. You may have initially expressed your own opinions against the superior knowledge of your abuser, and quickly learned that doing so invited him to intimidate you. This intimidation will gradually encourage you to abandon the very principles you grew up with. The very act of sensing that he is still in control is the main goal of the intimidation. To feel that he is still in control, your partner needs to stir you up and see what happens. Either you react as you are supposed to, and then he knows that you pose no threat, or you oppose or do something else that confirms to him that you are not fully controlled by him, which initiates another round of coercing and controlling actions.

When a client is asked how they would have responded to the abuse they are now suffering when they were younger, before they met their partner, they are all confident that they would not have tolerated it. They are also certain that they would have encouraged friends or family not to tolerate this behaviour either. This certainty is based on the realisation that when they were young women, before they met their long-term abuser, they would have seen that there is no place for abuse between intimates and, if it occurs, that the abuse is the sole responsibility of the abuser. Humans have a strong behavioural incli-nation (instinct) to cooperate; to the vast majority of humans, this is sensed as a clarity, an intrinsic part of your view of the world and your place in it. You came into the relationship knowing who you are and why you behave in certain ways, and knowing the principles and standards by which you want to live your life. You probably saw no reason for violence and abuse in human relationships, and would not condone the destruction of any human being. You were unlikely to accept disrespect and would be quick to apologise if you felt that you had hurt another person.

The male intimate abuser gradually removes that clarity, and you become anxious and confused. You see your confusion as a product of your naivety and your lack of understanding. You are unaware that the very basis for your decision-making, your facility for instinctive reaction, is unavailable to you. It is not that your instinct has disappeared but rather that it has been drowned out by the domineering and incessant voice of your abuser. You are out of touch with a core ability: you have gradually lost the ability to be yourself. This causes you extreme anguish and erodes any belief you had in your own integrity. You may even become convinced that you are not worthy of respect and that your helplessness is a result of your own stupidity. You lose the ability to make quick decisions and your animal brain becomes so quiet that your only response to danger is to freeze. You become like a rabbit caught in the headlights, unsure whether to run to the left or to the right. You may become inhuman in that you are like a robot without an inspiring mind, and you function only as you have been programmed to do by the abusive man in your life.

When I first met Norma, she found it difficult to accept that she had changed a great deal and that she was no longer the same woman that had taken over the role of her father when he died. When she was eighteen years old, she was called on to manage the family business. Her mother was ill and Norma was the eldest of the three children. Over the next ten years, she developed the family business while supporting the education of her siblings and caring for her mother. She married an intimate abuser when she was thirty-one and came to me when she was fifty. She believed that she was capable of changing her husband and wanted my help to get him to listen to her.

She described a horrendous relationship where she was never good enough and where her plans were criticised and her strategies undermined. She was stunned by her own answer when I asked her how often she had felt appreciated in her intimate relationship. Her clear response was that she had never felt appreciated and that she was sure that was true even before the marriage. She confessed that she had had many doubts before the wedding but that her family and friends had encouraged her to ignore them. When we both explored what she would have said to any of her friends who were being abused, she could remember telling her own sister to break off her relationship with a local man because Norma said that this man was like a spoiled child who threw tantrums if he did not get what he wanted.

Eventually, she came to recognise that she had married the same kind of man as the one she had identified earlier, one who was like a spoiled child. She recognised the tantrums of her husband as behaviours that were intimidating and violent when she resisted him. She cried when she realised that she had been seduced by his lies, and that his ability to blame her had led her to ignore his destructive behaviour. She admitted that she believed that her partner would eventually grow up and become the man that she wanted him to be.

Yet she knew deep in her soul that he had no interest in taking any responsibility for his actions. He lived on her income and worked intermittently for ten years. When he had his own money, he spent it on himself, and failed to contribute to the household budget. She disclosed that his mother had warned her of his selfishness when they were first married. She could recall the nagging voice of her own intuition, which she ignored, and which gradually went quiet. She wanted me to help her reason with her abuser, and believed that the glimmer of hope that she retained for the future could be fanned into a flame. She was scared of failure and of being trapped in a mental prison.

When she recognised what he had done to her, when she realised that she was no longer the decisive young woman who was capable of running a business, she became very angry at her stupidity and the fact that she believed that she had let him destroy her. It took all my experience to guide her into seeing that she had not cooperated in her own destruction. She and I spent some time examining her abuser: she agreed with me that he was an extremely cunning and selfish man and that he had hidden these traits from her when they first met. I tried to assure her that it didn't matter how competent she was, because once he had targeted her, this skilful abuser worked unseen, and nobody would have been able to explain what he was doing.

Norma is now living on her own. Her children have left home and she has started a new business. It is a pleasure to watch her regain her own effective talents. She is decisive and successful. She is also happy and fulfilled. She visits me on occasions to check in with me, in case she is going to be seduced by another skilled intimate abuser.

You are controlled

Once you are at the point with the intimate abuser where your sense of self is degraded and your access to your instinctive world is removed, he will introduce instructions and restraints, which will regulate your whole life. The degree of control is most often very big, and affects all, or almost all, aspects of your life. A minority of male intimate partners (Gottman, 2002) will allow the woman freedom to behave as she wishes when he has no need for her, but will expect her to respond immediately when he has a need to be served by her. Men who act like that seem to be a small percentage of abusers, but you may be unfortunate enough to be in a relationship with one of them. These men are very dangerous as they can lash out without prior warning. The partner of this kind of abuser lives on a knife-edge of fear, as she does not get any prior warning of an attack and has no idea when the next assault is imminent. She comes to believe that she has failed in her duty as a wife and partner and that she needs to respond more efficiently when she is called on. The constant attempts to anticipate the next demand results in her talking about him in her mind even when he is away from her, and allows him to dominate her thinking all the time.

If you are in relationship with an abuser of this kind, you may be both scared and angry. You will be scared because your partner is unpredictable and the violence used by him is unrelated to your resistance. You may be willing to concede to him in any way that he wishes, but he may continue to assault you and ignore your agreement. You may also be angry as you realise that his behaviour is irrational and that his violence is cruel and unnecessary. You may realise that his violence is more than just controlling, and that it may also be punishing and vindictive. An abuser of this kind has very little interest in his public status; you may have known before you met him that he could be violent. He is very hard to manage, as he sees himself as invincible and believes he can intimidate anyone. You will probably be unaware of how he spends his free time; some of these men come and go when it suits them. Because he is a rare type of intimate abuser, you will find it difficult to explain him to others, and most of your listeners will be slow to believe you. There are very few sanctions which will help change his behaviour, and the police may want him for other crimes. Any abuser of this kind who spends time in prison may emerge with a sense of revenge, and could be even more dangerous to you.

The vast majority of skilled abusers, described by Gottman (2008), are the ones who are constantly in the business of control. They check on the minutiae of your daily routine, and may even measure the mileage covered by you in your car. They are probably constantly phoning and texting you. They use your children to spy on you and get them to report any changes to your routine. They indicate their displeasure repeatedly, and demand understanding and sympathy for the anguish that you are causing them. They issue warnings through the tone of their voice or their facial expressions, or the speed with which they drive the family car.

This abuser will orchestrate the level of tension in the home by berating you for the imaginary slights that he claims you inflict on him. Any woman who is in a relationship with this more common type of coercive-controlling partner can usually see the signs of her increasing risk, and will intensify her attempts to de-escalate the tension. Most clients describe this behaviour as 'keeping the peace'.

If you are in an intimate relationship with a male abuser, you will engage in tactics of appeasement – which is one of the aims of these men. You will submit to his direction and concede to his opinion. This is what the abuser expects will happen before he initiates the process. He is confident of success because he is experienced enough to know the extent and type of appeasement that you will offer in any given circumstance. This knowledge is unique to an intimate relationship and is used repeatedly. The aim of this monitoring is to avoid stress caused by uncertainty. When you engage actively in appeasement, it is visible and obvious to him that you are not actively pondering blame or some other kind of threat to him.

While it may be useful to make a distinction between the two types of abusers, the reality is that if either type is unhappy with the quality or the speed of the appeasement, they can become aggressive and violent. They can also assault the woman if she shows any level of resistance. The severity of the assault by the more unusual kind of abuser may bear no relationship to the level of resistance shown by his partner. The severity of the assault by the constantly controlling abuser may be proportionate to the level of resistance offered.

The woman who lives with either type of abuser will know that she is being controlled. It may be difficult for you to decide which category best describes your partner, because the effect of either is similar on you. You will not know how you ended up under this level of total control. You will condemn yourself for being naive and foolish, and be angry with yourself that you paid no heed to your intuition. Most of my clients admit that their gut was issuing warnings from early on in the relationship. You may also blame yourself for not following your intuition. Instead, it would be better if you acknowledged the force that you are dealing with.

Like many of my clients, you may be convinced that your abuser is not very clever. Olivia was well educated and felt sorry for her partner, as he had left school early. She told me that her abuser was a bit slow and that he seemed to have a poor memory. She was forced to change her opinion when she began the process of separation and presented a detail of all her assets to his solicitor. About a week later, she got a very abusive phone call from her abuser. He wanted to know what had happened to a bank account which he remembered had been opened in her name more than ten years previously. Her astonishment was compounded by the fact that she had forgotten all about the particular account, and that it been unused for more than ten years – and that it contained less than €50.

A target-woman is not controlled because she is inadequate or stupid; she is controlled because she has been targeted by a skilled abuser. The tactics used by the man, and his ability to hide them, make the abuser a determined, focused and degrading force that goes unrecognised by his intimate partner and by those of us who observe the effects of this force. Another element of the control you experience can be best demonstrated by the ambivalence and tolerance that you encounter in your surroundings. If you are religious, you will find that the sexual priority of men is a requirement which all women are expected to acknowledge. If you listen to the media, you will find radio commentators, and even US presidential candidates, who promote the idea that once the woman has been consensually intimate, she loses the right to reject further advances. This social collusion supports every male intimate abuser, and sends a clear message to his intimate partner that the community around her will be slow to protect her and to sanction him. This is one of the most valid reasons you have for keeping your abuse secret.

You are carrying his voice

If you are a woman who has shared an intimate life with a skilled abuser, you will have a number of voices in your head. You will hear the critical voices of your youth, perhaps coming from your parents, teachers or siblings. You may also be familiar with the judgemental and condemning voices of the society in which you live. You may be able to recognise the cultural and religious voices that oblige women to take a subservient role. These voices may have already been there before you were seduced into beginning an intimate relationship. If they are already present, they allow the skilled abuser to piggy-back on their influence and to achieve dominant mind-control very quickly.

The main difference between cultures and religions is the speed with which an abuser can achieve control. If the prevailing culture supports arranged marriages, then his job is already half done. If the society is one where women are seen as unequal and different, all he has to do is expand the undermining effects of the voices which are already present. He will be relentless in reminding you of your second-class status, and will expand the existing voices into a cacophony of condemnation.

If you have been raised in a culture or a family where women and men have equal status, then the intimate abuser must access your own critical voice and encourage your criticism of yourself. He must listen to you as you reveal the traits that you dislike about yourself, and repeat and expand these dislikes until you feel inadequate. Once you have accepted his negative analysis, you will fail to appreciate your talents, and concentrate on rectifying the behaviours which you believe are ruining your relationship. His voice may not need to be loud, as you will tune into it anyway, in the hope that by paying attention to it, you may learn how to improve yourself and your relationship and make your partner happy. You may also listen to his voice with the intention of trying to understand his concerns and in the belief that, by anticipating his needs, you may be able to provide him with an adequate response.

This focused attention is present when you meet people who want to help you. While you may appear to agree with friends or therapists, you will be analysing their input against the opinions and instructions of your abusive partner. When you have heard what people like me have to say, you may dismiss my ideas and my suggestions as being the wrong solution for your problems. You will probably quickly revert to his voice and may even tell me that you cannot follow my suggestions because he would object to them. If I meet you on a number of occasions, you may let me know that you are unwilling to change your routine because you know that you would be at more risk if you did so.

Dee came to my office for help in dealing with her teenage children. During my initial assessment, I had a sense that her partner was unsupportive of her parenting. When we both explored her partner's behaviour, it was very apparent that she was living with a devious and skilled offender. She strongly resisted my tentative assessment and categorically stated that her husband had never beaten her. I met her for three sessions and made some suggestion that she might step back from parenting the oldest child. I tentatively put forward the idea that the father could take over the role. Her response was instant. She could not do so because it was her fault that the child was difficult; the father had warned her that unless she got her act together, he would report her to Child Protection Services. We explored how she came to believe this, and how she came to be so afraid.

She admitted that she spent most of her life trying to be a buffer between her husband and her children. She said she had no say in the family, and that her mind was full of the expectations and threats that her husband issued. Though she claimed not to have been beaten, she came to recognise that having his hand placed around her throat was more frightening than a punch on the face. She also came to realise that she was rejecting my tentative suggestions because she knew from the voice in her head that trying this approach would increase the risk to her and her children. Dee withdrew from therapy because she decided that it would be easier to put up with her abuser than to try and change her own thinking.

Many clients have been previously diagnosed as weak, confused, withdrawn, depressed, having borderline personality disorder, or even being psychotic, when the reality is that they are cut off from their own instincts. They are amazing women to have been able to survive in a world where their very core is undermined by the person who shares their bed. This mind-control is insidious and constant. Some of them, like Dee, will make choices that best suit themselves, even when you or I might think she is foolish. Dee did learn that she was not to blame for all the difficulties in her relationship, and she found relief in that.

You are scared and may even be terrified

When a woman who shares an intimate relationship with a skilled abuser comes to the office, she is invariably scared. She is afraid that she will not be understood, that she will not be able to explain herself adequately, that she will be seen as vindictive, and that she will betray her partner. This fear is what distinguishes the abused person from most of the men I meet who claim that their wives are abusive. These men want to betray their partners, and they want me to condemn the women in their lives. They want me to believe that the woman should be sanctioned, and they want **my** guidance as to what might be effective. They show no loyalty to the woman or to the relationship. They are not afraid of being with me; instead, they are confident that I will believe them and support their agenda.

I have met some men who are scared. These are men who live with mentally ill women and who struggle to contain the illness. The demeanour of these men is different, in that they want my help to support the women who are ill, and my guidance in minimising the effects on the children. They never want their wives sanctioned. They are similar to the controlled women in that they want the abuse to stop and the tension in the family to be diminished.

The partner of a male intimate abuser has another layer of fear that emerges after some time. You may be one of those women who is afraid that some of your children will grow up to repeat the patterns of their parents. You may be afraid that your daughters will go out into the world already manipulated by the father's arrogance into believing that the man in a relationship is entitled to priority. You may be anxious that your daughter might be seduced into an abusive relationship. You are probably very concerned that your daughter will be seduced or assaulted into being an abused object for some clever man.

You may also be scared that any of your sons will behave badly towards any girlfriend that they may have. You are likely to interpret any teenage disrespect or aggression as a sure sign that your son will be an intimate abuser, like his father. You may get called the same names by your son as are used by your partner. You will be condemned for the same faults and ignored for the same reasons. Even if this is the case, this imitating behaviour does not guarantee that your son will treat his intimate partner badly. The subtle and hidden tactics that underpin the behaviour of a skilled abuser are not learned but are innate to all of us, and the reason they are used in a destructive way by coercive controlling men is the fact that they compensate for lack of skill in order to reach the same goals in a balanced, equal way. Thus, your sons do not need to be taught how to use these behaviours, as they can apply them already. What your sons need to learn is that they do not have the entitlement to abuse anyone, and that their intimate relationships must be founded on sexual equality. Some young boys, and girls, will have such a profound sense of entitlement that they are hard to influence. As a mother, or non-abusive father, of course you can do no more than impress this truth on all your children, both daughters and sons. The most effective way of impressing your children is to demonstrate to them that you will not continue to tolerate being abused.

Added to all these concerns is the fear that your partner is beyond your reach. No matter how often you plead with him, no matter how often you forgive him, you are unable to change his attitude or his destructive behaviour. You are also unable to measure up to his continuously changing demands and his ever-increasing standards of perfection. You are possibly demoralised by his lack of sympathy for your distress and de-energised by his lack of appreciation for your efforts. You feel tired, and may have become depressed as a result of your continued failures and by the erosion of your hope. Your life is surrounded by instructions and threats which form the perimeter of your mental prison.

These feelings of anxiety, concern and fear are compounded by the growing realisation that you are unable to access your own inner voice. You may have begun to lose faith in your ability to think and to decide without checking with his voice. You probably find that a simple job, such as shopping for groceries, becomes a series of small decisions where you defer to his instructions and ignore your better judgement. You will be slow to avail of any spare time in ways that stray outside the boundaries that he has prescribed. You may not be able to visit friends or go to the cinema. You may spend much of your mental energy analysing every decision and checking it against his guidance. You will become gradually split, in a process that leaves you with no instinctive thoughts and permits you to operate only from your reflective mind. This reflection is not filled with your own reasoning but with the implanted thoughts, opinions and threats of your intimate partner.

You can become terrified by the effects of this split. You come to realise that you are no longer the vibrant and instinctive person that you once were. You see this division of your mind as some kind of madness; in fact, you are encouraged to do so by the abuser, who repeatedly tells you that you are losing your mind. Clients say that they can cope with being assaulted, that they can somehow accept being raped, but that they are unable to live with the continuous mental torture that marks their lives. Because the cause or the extent of this terror is hidden from you and most other abused women, you begin to see yourself as mentally flawed. You come to accept the male demarcation of your role because you have no base from which to challenge it. You will lose your self-esteem, your confidence and your ability to trust yourself. You will come to accept that the prison you are in is built on your own inadequacies, and the fear and terror you experience is your own fault. It seems reasonable to you, as the woman who lives with this persistent degradation, to deduce that if you are so inadequate, naive, supersensitive and mad, then you deserve all the distress you experience. The most terrifying thought you have may be that you are the cause of your own madness.

You are thought-controlled

All of the above effects – the sense of being trapped, the sensation of not being able to think, the feeling of being split off from your real instinctive self, the persistent sound of his voice, the anxiety for your children, and the acceptance of your self-inflicted madness – are the powerful effects of his coercive thought-control. These effects take place without your understanding, and certainly without your permission or collusion. The abuser will be persistent, devious, manipulative and deliberate in achieving his goal. He never gives you a break, and after some time you become unable to free your mind of his control. Because you have lost your ability to think flexibly, you are unable to protect yourself or to go on the offensive. You accept his opinion because you are unable to form your own. You accept the information he supplies because you lack either the energy or the courage to challenge him. You may even confess to things you did not do, so that he might leave you alone. You will be invited to share rituals and formalities that suit him, without any recognition that you find them distasteful. You may have engaged in demeaning and time-consuming tasks that make you feel degraded. You may have become convinced that no one will believe you, and have watched helplessly while he grooms your family, your friends and even the system that is supposed to protect you.

When coercive mind-control of this extent is established, you will go about your daily routine like a robot, and stay within the confines of your mental prison. You may cry out for help to cope, or for the abuse to stop, but you are probably unconvinced that any of us can be effective. You may also cry out for someone to make your partner happy, because you have failed to do so. But all of the attempts by society to meet your requests will founder on the arrogance and deviousness of your long-term abuser. If we were to meet a child who was being subjected to the above tactics, if we were to encounter a prisoner who was being tortured in this way, if we were to meet a person who was being thought-controlled by a cult or sect, we would know immediately that our first intervention would be to protect the person from further mind-control. But when we as a community encounter a skilled abuser and his intimate partner, we blame her and collude with him.

I have never encountered a case where my client was permitted by the courts to disengage from her abuser and never to speak to him again. Solicitors and judges all demand that clients engage with their abusers for the purposes of reconciliation, mediation or parenting. These demands show a real misunderstanding by these professionals of the experience of the woman, and of the tactics of the male intimate abuser. One of my aims in writing this book is to increase society's knowledge about coercive control in intimate relationships. As long as society looks away from very obvious signs of abuse, and the level of awareness of the less visible effects of coercive mind-control remains low, we must keep researching these issues. Alcoholism, a troubled childhood, or any other self-victimisation of the abuser cannot be excuses for abusive behaviour. Today, the awareness of how strongly entitlement is associated with partner abuse is slowly increasing, but there are as yet no effective psychological methods that can influence a male intimate abuser to give up his sense of entitlement.

The abused woman is convinced that the partner who has made her thoughts rigid and controlled will find a way to manipulate society so that he can remain abusive. Like all target women, your conviction is based on the firm evidence that, while this form of crime is endemic, few if any male intimate abusers are charged with these crimes, and only a tiny proportion of charges lead to sanctions. You will realise that you are not only a victim of your own adult abuser but a victim of a society which is still unable to identify and sanction the harmful behaviours of male intimate abusers as a group.

Chapter Five

The principal components of your steps to freedom

It is very likely that the information I will share with you will include thoughts that have already occurred to you as you grapple with the dilemmas of your relationship. Your intuition may initially have alerted you to the danger you are in, and you may have had doubts and uncertainties from an early stage in the relationship. You may even have been through periods when the relationship was suspended or when you did not want to formalise the bond. At times, you may regret some decisions that you thought you made freely, or the fact that your children make it more difficult for you to be free.

When you have tried to change your situation previously, it is likely that you have attempted to change your abuser, or your own actions towards him. You've tried to change him by being kind to him, by putting pressure on him, by begging him, or by influencing him in other ways. You've tried to change yourself by trying to understand him so that you can act differently, and thus change him, and the relationship, for the better. You may have tried talking therapy to become a better person, and you may have talked to friends about how you can do better. Also, it is most likely that your tactics never helped.

One reason for this is the fact that your abuser changes as you change. If you threaten to leave, he might start re-grooming you, which makes you want to give the relationship another chance. He might access your pity and your sympathy, and remind you of how sad his life is, and that he is unable to handle it without you. He might hand you the 'love-card' to make you feel special and wanted by him again, which raises your hope that this good feeling will stay. Or he might use threats or even violence. He might say that you are useless, and would not be able to handle life without him. He might say that he will hurt you – or your children, or pets – if you take any further step towards leaving. In sum, he uses his previously well-established mental control over you to tighten the ties even more. It is very likely that you have given up, and feel more helpless than ever, and possibly desperate, because you feel that you have nowhere to turn.

This is why I have found that to be effective and safe, your steps towards freedom must start from within. You must begin by dismantling the mental control your abuser has over you. The process of awareness, confirmation, autonomy and self-priority will gradually bring freedom and mental space in which you can move. I encourage you to start with the steps that I present here. When you begin to realise that he is controlling your emotions, and that he knows how to regulate your thoughts and feelings, you may become more afraid or more angry. You may need to be coached into seeing your partner's way of working without him realising that you are watching him. You can do this by continuing to behave as you have in the past. You can react to his conversations with the usual pleas or anxieties that you have always expressed, and you can allow yourself to engage with him in an attempt to educate him, if that is what you usually do.

A few words about communication

We human beings are programmed from birth to communicate. From when we are very small, we hear the voices of our parents, and perhaps our siblings, and our brains are wired to be attentive and, eventually, to communicate. Human beings, as well as many animals, are born to be members of larger groups, where communication is essential. When we are with another person, not communicating often feels awkward. Imagine a person who never responded to you: who sat in your kitchen and was silent, held their hands still and folded on the table, looked away, and had a slightly hunched body posture. You would soon become uneasy around that person. You would want to know what was wrong with them, and even whether they might pose a threat to you. That is why, when your abusive partner talks to you or acts in a pressing way that demands your attention, you are triggered to respond, as would any person in that situation. To stay silent and neutral in such a situation is against our nature. Furthermore, the abuser has gathered a profound knowledge of you, and what issues and themes will draw your emotional as well as your full cognitive attention. Thus, what he tells you will be heightening your focus in an extraordinary way. You may say that the abuser knows what makes your emotional alarm-bell go off. And because the cause of the alarm is so agitating, you react as if a fire had broken out. Would you be able to sit still and do nothing if the fire-alarms went off in your home? Almost certainly not. Would you be able to sit still if you smelt smoke and heard the roar of flames? Absolutely not. But with the abuser, and the fact that he has 'set off' your alarm, you will have to be alert to the possibility that the instant urge to respond might trigger even more fire within you. Holding back can, in some situations, be of more help than reacting, because the very act of responding, of defending yourself, of trying to explain, sets off emotions in you that not only tell your partner that you are still completely manageable by him, but also trigger the drive to be understood, to get your point across, to make him answer back in the right way. This is bound to lead nowhere. By engaging in this behaviour, you are much more likely to find yourself back on the downward spiral to even more anger, frustration, and (hopelessly) trying to communicate this to your partner. My suggestion is that you start by pondering what I write here, to see if it seems reasonable to you, and take your time before you make any changes. Do this at your own pace.

Section 1

I hope that the following sections will draw you into a process of awareness, confirmation, autonomy and self-priority. I want to remind you that, as you journey with me, the aim is not to advise you or to direct you. Rather, it is to encourage you to take the steps I describe below and get you to a place where you start to reclaim your instincts and your gut feeling. With the help of your own instincts and gut feeling, you may start to assess and decide on your preferred options. The remainder of your life can be one where you begin to make decisions that are yours, and in that freedom you will begin to recover your sense of clarity and your confidence.

Awareness

The most difficult and most painful part of the work I do with target women is to make them aware of the tactics used by their partner. The skill of the psychephile is based on his ability to hide his devious behaviours so that his target does not know what he is doing. This means that you have been seduced into a relationship with an abuser without knowing what is happening to you. You will be mystified when you find yourself immersed in a relationship that offers you little joy and demands your complete commitment, without any affection or appreciation in return. You may be angry with yourself for being gullible, naive or stupid for allowing any man to abuse you. You may have listened to your friends, who claim that if any man abused them, they would walk away. You will have heard and read media pundits who berate women like you for putting up with a man's violent behaviour. You probably feel less able than your sisters and friends, who seem to be able to manage their intimate relationships better than you do. You feel judged by a society that tolerates your partner's intimidation, minimises his violence and colludes in his control.

Living in a mental prison, you have no idea how he managed to put you there. You may not even realise that you are in an abusive situation, and may believe that your distress is normal. You may be convinced that you went into the prison voluntarily, and that it is your own fault that you cannot cope with your surroundings and your tortured life. You will find it difficult to accept that you had no role to play in your dilemma and that it does not matter what you did previously or what you do in the future in an attempt to change your abuser. You will find it unbelievable that your partner has used all the principles by which you have lived your life in order to strengthen his control over you, and to drain you of your energy. Like most clients, you will be stunned to be told that your kindness, loyalty, sympathy and commitment have been the very traits that attracted the abuser to you. You will find it difficult to comprehend the idea that he has worked on you in a deliberate and calculating way. It is beyond your understanding that the man you fell in love with was intentionally making sure that he could control you from the day you met him.

Anyone who attempts to bring these issues to your consciousness will need to be respectfully persistent. While you need time to talk about what has happened to you, it is not good enough to listen to your own analysis of your situation and to engage in support or problem-solving, without challenging the work which has already been done, covertly, by your abuser. In order to begin to unravel the debilitating effects that your partner has caused, I need to unravel his tactics. If your friends minimise or deny that your partner's persistent behaviours have resulted in him controlling your thoughts, I know you will find it difficult to accept that he has been doing so from the start of your relationship. You will find it very hard to believe that all your attempts to keep the peace, or to diminish the tension between you, only worked when it suited him, and that if you were consistent in your response, he was equally inconsistent in his demands. In other words, when you had finished solving a problem, he moved the goalposts so that your efforts were no longer satisfactory.

His needs kept changing, and his level of satisfaction kept decreasing, until you got to a stage where you became convinced that nothing you did would be good enough. It is important for me to raise these tactics, and the agenda that he follows, so that I can elaborate on them with you. I try to offer you my information, my point of view, without pushing you to accept it.

The task for those who listen to victims and survivors is to effect a gradual, self-directed and positive change in their thinking. This change can only occur if each woman does this in her own way and in her own time. Such a change in thinking will not begin unless the woman is able to begin to discard the explanations she has carried about the intimidation, abuse, violence and rapes which their abusers have committed during the relationship. These women need to be encouraged to move their focus away from their own inadequacies and be helped to examine the behaviours of their abusers.

Though some therapists or friends may be able to achieve this change of focus readily with some target women, most often the change demands time and skill. The goal is to repeat the efforts to raise awareness and to delay engaging in solutions until the client is in agreement with the analysis. A therapist or counsellor cannot demand that you accept my explanations because, in doing so, we will just be adding to the control that you already experience.

You may be attending some therapist who wants to help you to regain your own thoughts. The journey is not easy, and may open up some areas of your experience which you may have hidden from yourself. This requires that the therapist or counsellor acknowledge that the awareness I am pursuing may be even more painful for you than the sense of denial and shame that you already carry. It is like a physician inflicting pain in order, eventually, to achieve relief. I am obliged to acknowledge this process and the courage involved in engaging in it. I need to tell you repeatedly that I do not want to impose my solution on your life. I do not want to replace the control of your partner with the control of the system. But I need to be very aware that this is easier said than done, and that, in order to be a guide, and not another controller, we therapists or counsellors need to constantly monitor our work. In our anxiety to protect, we may issue instructions and make demands on women whose lives are already compromised by instructions and demands.

I cannot pretend that I am able to change the abuser or to protect a client from further abuse, but I can make it my mantra that my work with every target-person should only be about ending the mind-control that the partner has achieved. I was very challenged in my early career by a client who said that she felt as though she was coming to WeightWatchers when she stepped into my office. She had felt that I had an agenda for her to follow, and that I had a weekly target for her to achieve. This client gave me invaluable knowledge about my lack of clarity and my anxiety with regard to her safety, which I depended on her to soothe. I must strive not to put pressure on clients; the mantra I learned could be used repeatedly until I am confident that the client and I are cooperating in ways that give her an equal say in the process, and complete autonomy in her decisions.

As you read these paragraphs, you may begin to realise that the journey to your mental freedom will require courage, commitment and skill. You will need to be brave, because all change is difficult and risky. My aim is to help you reach clarity: I do not judge what you subsequently decide to do. Some women remain in their abusive relationships in the belief that they would not survive without their partners. It may be that they also believe that their partners will change. Some women are convinced that their partners would not survive without them.

If you make your choice from a position of clarity, and without fear, you will find that you will be able to cope with the outcome of your own decision.

Section 2

Confirmations

Many people who are subjected to abuse struggle with the process of awareness, and feel that it is unfair to scrutinise the behaviour of others. You may believe that, by analysing the behaviour of your partner, you are forming a judgement of him that goes against your principles. You may be reluctant to scrutinise *him*, but I invite you to scrutinise his conversations and his actions. It can be very difficult to recognise that your partner can be normal and sociable to everyone else and yet devious and callous, and act cruelly, in the intimacy of your relationship.

It may take some time for you to begin to recognise the tactics and intentions of your partner. It can be helpful if you begin to tell yourself that the effect of his behaviour is deliberate. When he wants you to be confused, he will challenge your thinking. When he wants you to be embarrassed, he knows how to do so, because you have told him. When he wants you to be afraid of him, he acts in ways that you have told him make you afraid. If he wants to terrify you, he will repeat threats that he knows already have that effect. The task becomes one of observation, persistence and encouragement. You will need to observe his behaviour and note its effect on you.

A woman who can begin to change her focus needs to be encouraged by examining what she is learning, and the value of that learning in her own life. When you begin to accept that the feelings you carry are deliberately engendered by him, and recognise his ability to monitor and dictate these feelings, you begin to realise that he has deliberately colonised your thinking to make you easy to control. You will become aware that he knows how you think and how you will react to any suggestion from him. You can begin to see how he pushes your buttons, in the knowledge that he knows how you will be affected, and how you will react. You will learn that he can manipulate your emotional existence as he chooses, and that he can penetrate any protection that you had used to shield your thoughts. You will eventually accept that you are suffering from something that has dismantled your emotional barriers and is continually putting your psychological health at serious risk.

This sense of awareness, and the confirmation of the way in which he operates, brings a huge sense of relief to every abused woman, as she realises that she had no role to play in her distress. The relief is enhanced by the knowledge that it was his deviousness, and not her stupidity, that facilitated the thought-control. When you begin to accept that everything he has told you was untrue, or at least designed to make himself look good, you will learn that your appreciation of the truth has been used against you, and that your honesty has given him access to your thought-processes. When you observe how your kindness and your commitment have been directed to his benefit, you will see why you are frustrated and drained of energy. You may also learn that your abuser is incapable of showing genuine appreciation, that all his words of devotion are designed to seduce you into ignoring his bad behaviour, and that his promises to change have been broken. With a strong need to control and punish, your coercive-controlling partner has no intention of keeping his promises.

Many of my clients have been told that they are vital to their abuser, and most of them believe that these men would not be able to live without them. The harsh truth is that your services are needed, for the reasons I have laid out before, but that you personally are not. Certainly, an abusive person can become obsessed with you and what you do, and is very likely to do so. Still, the lack of desire to consider many different aspects of other things in his life corresponds with your partner's lack of interest in considering many aspects of you. Like some of my clients, you may find it easy to remove yourself from the intimacies of the bedroom, but many find it hard to abandon the role of mother which the abuser also demands. Because the woman's experience of degradation and helplessness is most often felt in the bedroom, most relationships start to change when she no longer shares her bed with her abuser. But like other abused women, you may have been encouraged to adopt other roles, such as mother and something of a slave, which you may feel obliged to maintain as part of your initial commitment to him. As a woman of your word, you may find it extremely difficult to withdraw completely from a relationship to which you have agreed to commit for life.

It may take considerable time, and persistent dehumanising, for you to arrive at any decision that would terminate your role as partner to your abuser. This time-span can make the job of your therapist difficult, and is misunderstood by most professionals. From an outside perspective, it may seem that you are inactive or frozen, as a result of a sense of foreboding. What you may be doing is actually grieving the loss of your dream, and mourning your failure to listen to, or even to hear, your own voice. This process of sadness and darkness brings with it a feeling of guilt that is difficult to explain. You know that the relationship is harmful for you but, in your kindness, you retain feelings of concern and affection for your abuser. You probably have no interest in having him sanctioned, and would much prefer it if there was a way to modify his behaviour and end the abuse directed towards you.

Sometimes a woman may be so enmeshed in the relationship that she is unable to see the tactics which are employed by her abuser. She may be so enamoured of him, or so forgiving of him, that she wants to think the best of him. It can be useful to draw this woman's attention to how her partner manipulates her friends or her children. If you cannot identify the ways in which he deliberately controls you, you may be able recognise the tactics he uses to influence others. You may be aware that he lies about you to others. You may have observed how he grooms others to side with him against you. If you have a number of children, you may notice how he treats each one differently. You may notice that he supports some or all of the children against you. You may observe the grooming of some of your children, and not others. You might be familiar with his strategy of divide-and-conquer, which results in your family and friends being unhelpful to you. You may be aware of your feelings of isolation, and your uncertainty with people with whom you were previously comfortable.

Bringing all this to your attention may help you to recognise that you have been subjected to many years of the same tactics. You will also become convinced that your partner is self-centred, and that his primary agenda is to get what he needs without consideration for others. This selfishness is anathema to you, and you will find it hard to rationalise how anyone could be so preoccupied with himself. The message from your youth may be that you should love your neighbour, and your personality and your nature demand that you do what you can in that regard. Sadly, the message is badly delivered and grossly misunderstood. What the religions of the world encourage is that we should love and care for ourselves in the same way as we do for others. The implication of this universal message is that, if we do not care for ourselves, we will do a poor job of caring for others.

SECTION 3

Autonomy

For some women, taking charge of her own decisions may be a strange and difficult process. Some women grow up as independent thinkers but, like most women, you may have been reared in a time when men made all the big decisions, or with people who allowed you to make decisions and then criticised you for the outcomes. You may be a people-pleaser, and would like to make decisions that keep everyone happy. Like most kind people, you may feel obliged to explain all your decisions so that people will agree with your actions. Your abusive partner will latch on to any weakness, which will allow him to challenge your own reasoning. You may have lost contact with your immediate decision-making ability, and your slow (analytical) decision-making abilities might have become skewed. You may continuously reject the idea that you can restore your own faculties, and will be confused and hesitant about any decision that you cannot share with him. It takes a firm and encouraging persistence on the part of the professional with whom you are working, to help you begin to make small and easily hidden decisions that do not put you at risk of further abuse. These little decisions, made and evaluated by you, become the chinks of light that open up your own internal life and bring back to you the ability to think that has previously been hidden from you.

You may have been raised in a culture or a religion that facilitates the behaviour of the abusive man in his efforts to control the mind of his intimate partner. This upbringing encourages women to be kind and forgiving, and to try to see the good in people, and to ignore their failings. It will encourage you to resist the idea that your partner could be as devious, calculating and destructive as he is. The idea that you can stand on your own and make valid decisions about yourself and your children may never have occurred to you. One of the ways in which you can be encouraged to overcome your hesitancy is to invite you to examine how, and why, your partner maintains his control. Instead of trying to anticipate his needs, I invite you to focus on what his intention might be, and what effect he deliberately achieves. This focus can be difficult for you, and I would encourage you to remain cautious that this new awareness remains hidden from your abuser.

Though this work may appear time-consuming and may require your therapist to delay their instinctive desire to solve the crisis, we all need to build any momentum on the solid foundation of your own rational thinking, and timing. If you rush into making decisions, or if I, as your therapist, impose my own decisions on you, it is probable that your efforts will fail, and that you will be plunged into further recriminations about your own stupidity. It is very common that clients have a sense of great failure after years of therapy, because in spite of the good intentions of their therapist, they remain in a life with which they cannot cope. They see this as a failure of themselves and not as a sign of the way society, and in extension many professionals, do not understand partner abuse.

This sense of failure may also haunt you, if you try to solve the problem of your relationship without examining either what is really going wrong, or that you have very little influence on your abuser. I do not pretend to have magic powers, or to be able to prescribe an instant solution to the problem. Helping you locate and examine the tumour that is slowing killing your spirit will encourage you to isolate the real problem in your life. My wish is that you would decide what to do with this tumour, once you know what it is. I would like you to know what influence it has had on you. When you and I have come up with a reasonably accurate diagnosis, I will respect and support any decision you wish to make about your future. If you decide on an intervention or follow-up treatment, or both, I would encourage you to do so without explaining your plans to anyone. Very few people understand the reality of your experience, and there might be people around you who will not allow you to be yourself.

Many therapists find themselves getting into a crisis-solving position with their abused clients. The idea that a woman is returning to a home where she may be assaulted or raped naturally makes the therapist anxious. The expectation that the abuse will compromise any children in the household may lead the therapist to activate a community response before it is beneficial to do so. The reporting of risk may help the therapist to feel competent when it may in fact only exacerbate the abuse of the woman. The desire to eliminate the problem may encourage the therapist to act independently of the woman. The skill and persistence that is required when dealing with a woman who is mind-controlled demands that I unravel the effects of his tactics before I invite the woman to activate her own solution. There is an ethical and practical demand that all of us must be proactive if there is a serious risk of harm to any family member.

I accept that there may be a clear and present risk to your life which supersedes any form of therapy. Though legislation varies in different countries, it is almost universally required that the rule of limited confidentially applies in cases of high risk. In many countries, therapists are obliged to respond to high-risk situations by cooperating with statutory bodies in creating a barrier that protects vulnerable adults and children. It requires a high degree of skill to make this assessment; even with all the skill and experience of a good therapist, it is impossible to do so with certainty. It is very useful if I acknowledge that you have survived in the relationship for a long time, and if you believe that you can handle him, or mind yourself, I may need to accept your own risk assessment. If you are distraught because of an escalation of the risk, then I may need to be proactive with regard to your immediate protection. High-risk cases can escalate into lethal events if the person is not given protection. Your life, and those of your children, are sacred, and deserve to be preserved as effectively as possible. The community needs to respond robustly when the abuser is using extreme force. Early in my career, using all the assessment tools available to me, I concluded that a client was at risk but that there was no urgent danger. I failed to discern the anxiety that she portrayed in her demeanour as she sought to reassure me that she would come back to my office in one week. She was murdered that night by her abuser.

My aim is to give my clients the right to live their own life. This right has been usurped by the abuser. One of my current clients has spent more than eighteen years being treated as a non-person and being subjected to demeaning and demoralising tasks which have defined her role within her relationship. When a client is asked who they really are, some say that they do not know. When they are asked who they were before the abuse, they describe a capable and energetic woman. This may also be who you are, but you may be cut off from your abilities and your energy. I would like to encourage you to regain your real self, which is not lost but only hidden. There is a part of your being which has not been damaged by your abuser, and I believe that this is the part of you that will start your recovery process. By reading books like this, you are already on the right road, and I compliment you on every step you take towards reclaiming your autonomy. I would like to try to help you identify your real self, the person that you were before you were abused. I invite you to talk about your positive traits when you were free to be yourself. I would like you to think about a time when you were living your own life, and how your kindness, loyalty and truthfulness were important to you. I would like you to admire these attractive traits, and recognise that your goodness was what drew your abuser to you. It may take some time for you to convince yourself that you have the ability to live a useful and free life.

Section 4

Becoming the priority

In the intimacy of your relationship, you have a list of priorities. You probably place your abuser at the top of that list. You may have your children in second place, and may even have them graded in terms of their needs. If you have a career or a part-time job, you are likely to regard your responsibilities to your employer as important. If you have parents or siblings who are struggling, you may try to be available to them. When I ask you where you are on this list, you will probably become hesitant and a little confused. You cannot answer immediately because it is a question that you may not have asked yourself before.

If I was to invite you to put yourself first, you may react with disbelief and uncertainty. You do not believe that putting yourself first is a legitimate thing to do. What is more disturbing is that you might readily admit that you do not know how to do it. You might think that I am inviting you to become somewhat like your abuser and that you will become selfish. I do not expect you to become self-centred but to prioritise your own care so that you will be better able to care for those you love.

It takes some persistence from me to show you that if you put yourself first, you will be better able to respond to the legitimate needs of others. It is difficult for you to accept that making yourself a priority in your own life is the right thing to do. Getting you to care for yourself so that you can be better at caring for others can help you understand that being self-aware can be a good thing if the purpose is not to benefit yourself only, but also to benefit others. As you review the behaviour of your abuser, you will identify the many selfish tactics which are designed to benefit him. You will learn that the behaviour itself is not as destructive as the intention that accompanies it. The intention is to control you by draining you of your energy, and to make you compliant and without hope.

If I were to suggest that you take a little time for yourself each day, you probably feel that you are not entitled to do so. Your day is filled with responsibilities and tasks that must be done to his satisfaction, and you know that if you took time for yourself, you would feel guilty if he was not happy with the results of your efforts. You also know that, if he found out that you were caring for yourself, he may become angry and punish you. If I was to ask you when you last had a holiday away from all your responsibilities, you will probably admit that you have seldom, if ever, been away on your own.

Sometimes I have declined to take a fee from a client, and suggested that she spend the money on a treat for herself instead. If I check at the next session, I will probably find that she spent the money on something that other people wanted. She may even admit to me that she would be ashamed to spend money on herself. Like many, or indeed most, clients, you will want to convince me that the needs of others are a priority in your life, and that it is unnecessary for you to treat yourself. You may go so far as to try and persuade me that you can survive without treats, and that all you ever crave is peace. You would probably suggest that if your abuser found out that you had been good to yourself, you would pay the price of heightened tension, which would far outweigh any initial benefit to you.

It may be possible for some people to live without treats. But I believe that contented people are rewarded in some other way. They are supported and feel useful, and they are allowed to have their own opinions and thoughts. They may even get occasional gifts of items that they need, or some other acknowledgement of the efforts they are making. I call this the process of being appreciated: as all of us get older, we realise that it is appreciation that gives us the desire to continue to honour our responsibilities. Personally, I regard appreciation as the fuel that replenishes my energy.

If you have been living with a skilled abuser for a number of years, you are drained of your energy, and you may be starting to believe that you cannot go on for much longer. I will try to draw your attention to the lack of appreciation in your life, and to invite you to consider what it would be like if your abuser showed some genuine appreciation of your efforts. Most clients are unclear as to how that might happen, as their only experience is of insincere manipulation that is designed by the abuser to get him what he wants. I am sure you can accept that children, especially teenagers, may be reluctant to show appreciation, but even an occasional 'thank you' can make a parent feel better and give him or her the energy to keep going.

If you have few sources of appreciation in your life, I will encourage you to appreciate yourself. This way of thinking may be strange to you, and my initial approach is to give you permission to appreciate yourself. You probably feel that it is unhealthy to be proud of your achievements, and you may be unaccustomed to even examining your own efforts in a positive light. You may dismiss the exercise as wasteful and suggest that this kind of self-examination will not be of benefit in your life. You may want solutions to your problem, which you believe is caused, at least in part, by your own inadequacies. Like other clients, you are probably more comfortable in condemning yourself, and demonstrating how incapable you are of maintaining a peaceful relationship and a contented partner.

Steps to Freedom

I would like you to begin to list your most impressive achievements. Your most important achievement is that you are alive. Though you may be reluctant to admit it, you are living with a man who is capable of killing you if he felt he could get away with it. Being alive is complemented by the fact that, in spite of his mind-control, you are still sane. Along with these amazing achievements, you are probably also running a household and maybe holding down a job. Whatever faults you may have – and we all have some – you deserve praise and recognition for your strength, restraint and loyalty. The strength on which you draw seems to be boundless: even though you may acknowledge that you are coming to the end of your resources, I am certain that you are reluctant to give up the struggle, and that you still hope for a successful outcome for your partner, your children and yourself.

You may wish to invite me to help you persevere, in the hope that I can teach you ways of 'getting through' to your partner. You may encourage me to talk to him directly, as you admit, sadly, that all your talking has had no impact on him. Your restraint is apparent in the fact that you may never have called the police, or if you did, you did not pursue a charge. You have been assaulted and seduced, intimidated, and perhaps even raped by the man with whom you sleep. You are obliged to anticipate and administer to his needs, while ignoring the emotional cost to yourself. You have forgiven him repeatedly, and declined to seek revenge. You may have no interest in having him punished, but you do want him to change. You have been carried on a tide of false hopes and broken promises, and yet you may be prepared to give him another chance.

In some cases, if all else fails and all your hope is extinguished, you may abandon your restraint and resort to violence. Any woman who reaches that state of distress can sometimes be willing to be very dangerous, as she will be likely to use a weapon to inflict pain. While this action is rare, it has been used by many abusers to condemn the woman, and to gain sympathy for himself. It is hard to accept, but we might all revert to the use of violence if we are pushed hard enough. The majority of clients are also loyal, both to their abusers and to their relationships. They maintain that their abusers are good men with occasional bad habits. They list his explanations and excuses, in the belief that others will not condemn him. My clients tell me that if I met the abuser, I would probably see that he is not that bad, and that I would side with him and acknowledge that the problem is one of mutual inadequacy, or is entirely her fault. This loyalty is admirable, as is your desire not to expose the truth of his aggression and abuse. I salute your commitment to your relationship, and only ask that you transmit some of that commitment to your own well-being.

Though many therapists try to define this level of caring as being an unhealthy trait in any abused woman, seeing it as a form of co-dependency, I view it as a result of the commitment given by all helpful and loyal women. What is unhealthier is the use that the psychephile makes of this caring attitude, and the fact that your honesty and endeavour goes unrecognised and unrewarded. It is difficult, but very worthwhile, to begin to realise that while it is damaging for you to be thought of as controlled, it is even more damaging for the abuser to continue to deliberately abuse you. The cumulative effect of his achievements, and the growing arrogance that accompanies them, are a poison in the spirit of the man, and erode the good that you initially thought you saw in him. The longer he pursues his selfish agenda, the harder it becomes for him to save himself. When you recognise that the abuse is destroying him, you may decide to take a position where you are no longer available to be abused.

I believe that the most effective intervention is to use your own thoughts and ideas, which you have hidden from sight, and to encourage you to bring them forward. I acknowledge that you are the expert in your own safety, and I will agree to work with you to achieve a life where you are free of abuse. You may find yourself caught between my supportive voice and the voice of your partner. If that happens, you will feel pulled and dragged between us. As you spend far more time with your abuser, it is inevitable that his voice wins out: even though you may admit to seeing merit in my suggestions, you will realise that you are reluctant to follow them. You may even acknowledge that you attempted to introduce some of these changes, only to be seduced or intimidated into returning to your old ways. Any pressure and control I might bring to bear on you is simply replacing one form of control with another. My intention is always to do our best to refrain from that. Progress is not achieved by empowerment, as you have your own power. This change has already started to happen, and has got you to read this book, and maybe to seek help from a professional. This seed of change needs to be both nourished and protected. When you are putting yourself first, you can be encouraged to take some time to recognise how wonderful you are.

The task of guiding you through the steps of awareness, confirmation, autonomy and self-priority is not one that happens in a straight line; rather, bits of it happen at different times. It is the task of the therapist to monitor the journey, and to highlight the learning that the client is making. This can be slow and painstaking work, but it is well rewarded when you have what can be described as a lightbulb moment. The work is also complicated by the variety of women that are encountered in many different scenarios. You may be a woman who has never looked for help; you may be a woman who wants your relationship to work; you may be a woman who wants peace and quiet; or you may be a woman who has tried several remedies but who is still imprisoned. I would encourage you to take your time, and not to condemn yourself for not following the same pattern or timescale as some other target women. You are at a major crossroads in your life, and you can rest there for a while until you decide which path to follow. My sincere wish is that you do not go backwards, and that your path forward will be one that you will choose freely.

Part 2

Chapter Six

Steps 1-5: Awareness

I have set out some practical ways in which you can reverse the process that the psychephile uses. These are the steps that I encourage my clients to consider. I do not claim that they are unique, or that they are the only way to set your mind free. But after years of practice, I have learned that there is no quick-and-easy solution to the power, persistence and malevolence of a psychephile; this view corresponds with the clinical and personal experience of many professionals and targets. Though I have written the steps in roughly the chronological order that I use in my work, you may pick and choose to use from the steps in any way that is safe for you. You may wish to go back and forward through the range of suggestions, and you may choose to ignore some of my suggestions because you know better what might be good for you. You might find it useful to use some of the later steps first, and then revisit some of the earlier steps. My experience, however, is that the awareness steps are the single most powerful methods to incite change, and frequently revisiting a few steps at the time will help you build on previous knowledge and gain new experience, which will further enhance your chances of achieving full clarity and empowerment.

The abuser's persistent abuses and repeated lies are the scaffolding around your life. I hope my steps will let you see that scaffolding, and place yourself outside of its bars.

Steps

1. Keep your thoughts to yourself

He stores information about you

When you try to recall what you have told your abuser about yourself, you will begin to see that he has stored a huge amount of information about you. Even though it appears that he is not listening, he usually pays close attention to you. He hears things about you but does not respond in any normal way to the information. When you tell him that you are embarrassed, hurt or scared, he will not try to soothe you but will heighten your distress and hold you responsible for being naïve, stupid or over-sensitive. He may persuade you that what he is doing is normal, and that if you understood him, you would not be so anxious. He can push all your buttons and manipulate your emotions by using his store of knowledge about you. You may also have told him what makes you feel good or safe; he then sets out to remove these things from your life.

He uses your revelations, and those of others, against you

He gathers up any pieces of information that others may have shared with him about you. Your parents or siblings might tell him about any phobia that you may have had when you were growing up. They may tell him some family secret that he uses against you. They may reveal your school reports and your exam results. Your friends may tell him about some of your previous relationships. He may also find out from others if you have any physical weakness, or if anyone in your family had mental-health issues.

When he gets to learn aspects of your personality, or stories from your past that make you feel inadequate, he will bombard you with issues that demean you. As I have already mentioned, if you have had previous sexual partners, he will want to know the detail of these relationships, and will use this information to criticise your sexual behaviour while with him. If you have a child from a previous relationship, he will use the child's existence, or their behaviour, as proof of your failure to live up to his standards. If he finds out that you have had a miscarriage or an abortion, he will use this knowledge to increase your guilt and shame. He will blame all these difficulties on your sexual inadequacies, and make you feel almost lucky to have any man to share a bed with you.

If you stop feeding his store of knowledge, he will begin to lose influence

His ability to control your mind is founded on the information you have shared with him about your thoughts, hopes, dreams and anxieties. If you deny him access to your thoughts, he will not be able to influence them. You will gradually diminish the conversations you have with him in your mind, until you will eventually have your own thoughts, which are not being measured against his opinions. You can develop the skill of talking without saying anything important, or you can hide behind uncertainty and confusion. He will be pleased to observe that you have lost the ability to think clearly – which has been his objective since the day he met you.

He grooms others to tell him things about you

It might also be useful not to share your thoughts with others. Your children, your extended family and your friends are likely to be put under pressure by your abuser to give him any information that they may have about your thoughts or plans. Talking to yourself about your own life is best done in private; this will allow you to make up your own mind about what you wish to do. Getting suggestions even from the people who love you may leave you confused, as nobody knows what your life is like, and how devious your abuser is. Your friends and family may think they are being helpful if they alert him to your plans. They may believe that, if he knew what you were thinking, he might make an effort to improve. These well-meaning people do not understand how your abuser thinks, and they do not know of his deviousness.

You are talking to yourself about him

You may notice that you carry his voice in your head, and that most of your internal monologues develop into silent discussions with this voice. You may find yourself having an idea, and immediately tell yourself that he would not agree with that, or that you could never tell him that, or that you will need to pick a time when you can share the thought with him, in the hope that he will not get angry. These internal conversations are possible because you know what he thinks, and you are beginning to believe that he is seldom wrong. These conversations cause you to disqualify your own intuition and eventually convince you that you have very few good ideas. When you begin to think like that, you have become a victim of the most powerful form of mind-control. Nobody has the right to invade your mind in this way.

Your conversation is his battleground

It may also help you when you realise that you deserve some privacy in your intimate relationship. You are probably aware that your thoughts are never encouraged and that your opinions are never appreciated. It can be devastating to be living with a man who seldom says that you have had a good idea, and who never concedes that you are right. Being denigrated constantly is one of the most painful experiences of every woman who shares her life with a psychephile. Your ideas and opinions are valid, and deserve to be acknowledged. When you share your thoughts with your abusive partner, you are giving him further ammunition to use against you. Some of my clients describe this painful experience as 'having their buttons pushed'. He can accurately locate these buttons because you will have told him which ones hurt you. It seems as if any information of emotional value you display about how you feel and think serves as a trigger for your partner, and makes them want more. Strive towards not feeding him, but at the start of the process, in order to stay safe, you should begin by observing his behaviour, to see if you find that this seems true. Always strive to feel as safe as possible, whenever you take a step towards change that people around you can notice.

2. Stop listening to your abuser's message
He uses words first in the process of control

The process of mind-control is primarily a verbal one: even the assaults and rapes are accompanied by a tirade of words, before, during and after the act. Sometimes the tirade of abuse is sufficient without any actions, and you are intimidated and controlled by his language or his tone. You may be one of the women who are seldom or never physically assaulted, but the conversations you have had with your abuser make you feel obliged to do as he wishes. The process by which he establishes the terms and conditions of your relationship is one where he gradually tells you what he expects from you. These expectations are enforced by placing the responsibility for them with you, and by blaming you when these terms are breached. He may be a poor timekeeper but, if he expects punctuality from you, he will excuse himself when he is late but will not accept your explanation if you are late. These terms and conditions are presented and pursued in such a way that you will spend your time examining your own behaviour, in the mistaken belief that, if you eliminate your faults, you will be able to improve your relationship.

While establishing the terms and conditions of your relationship, he also begins the verbal process of grooming you. He will seduce you into having a range of feelings towards him. He may tell you that he loves you and cannot live without you. Although he is incapable of loving anyone but himself, you may find yourself wanting to love him. He may tell you that he has had a hard life, and you will begin to feel sorry for him. He may tell you that he is unable to communicate properly and that his temper gets the better of him sometimes, and you will learn to forgive him. While you are being groomed, you will also become aware of a level of fear that he generates, even though he seldom makes specific threats.

He is more verbal than you

You may have found yourself repeatedly wondering why you let yourself be drawn into circular conversations that end up in a criticism of you, or a threat from him towards you. You may hear things through your children that make you upset, or you may hear your friends repeating criticisms that he has initiated. Hearing another person repeating his condemnation of you, or hearing your children using a similar tone and language as their father, can be more hurtful than when your abuser said it. He can be very verbal when it suits him, but he may also withdraw from conversation for an extended period of time. This silence can be intimidating, and you will feel a growing sense of tension and anxiety, wondering when, and how, it will end. A confident and arrogant psychephile may use this tactic to force you into an apology and to encourage you to behave in ways that might avoid this period of silence in the future. Although we communicate best by means of language, the psychephile has many other ways of letting you know that he is not satisfied with your performance. These non-verbal communications can be more powerful in the intimacy of your relationship and, by being repeated on a regular basis, they can build up to a crescendo. People who do not live with your abuser will find it difficult to believe that his apparently common behaviours can have such a powerful effect on you. They do not understand that this man, who says he loves you, in fact wants to destroy your mind, and that he has invaded your thinking in subtle ways.

He says things that he does not mean

Most abused women never hear anything comforting from their partners. Though you may not be able to explain it, you will find yourself questioning his motives when he appears to be behaving in a loving way towards you. You may realise that his niceness is part of his way of getting what he wants from you. You may also begin to notice that you are seldom given what you would like, but are expected to be grateful for what he is doing or saying. Every psychephile is an expert at telling useful lies. He lies in a way that improves his own position. Your abuser uses your love of truth to persuade you that he is truthful too. It is difficult for you to believe that most, if not all, of the essential things he told you were either lies, or twisted versions of the truth.

You have heard enough of his criticism

You may come away from all such conversations feeling more unheard, more degraded and more afraid than you were before. If you are familiar with these feelings, there is very little point in hearing more of the same. You may be ready

73

to admit that you are scared of how well your abuser knows you, and that it frightens you when he seems to know what you are thinking. You may accept that he can draw you into discussions where you know you are going to lose your opinion, and where his ideas are paramount. He has bombarded you with his superior wisdom by wearing down your own instinctive knowledge. He has stripped you of your emotional reasoning, and can regulate your feelings in whatever way he chooses. It will be of benefit to you if you can begin to resist being drawn into these conversations in an active way. This might mean that you tell him to shut up – but doing so might put you at further risk.

Do not absorb his words

A more protective approach might be to develop the skill of hearing but not listening. When he speaks to you or texts you, his intention is to upset you. If you become upset, he has achieved his goal. He has little or no interest in you or your children, but he is fully focused on driving you mad. You can pretend to be upset, angry or confused, as this will please him. In reality, you can identify his motivation, and decide that you will not allow him to drive you mad. Because you have been targeted, in part because of your truthfulness, you may find it difficult to lie convincingly, but saying that you are in full agreement with him will please him most. This may also cause him to become confused – which may limit his tactics. You can use the same kind of skill I told you about as a reading advice. Practice refocusing from his actual words, and instead try to notice how his voice, his words and his actions make you feel. If they make you feel very afraid, or put down, or going crazy, this is the intention of your partner. Do not confront him. This is a safety measure. Keep your observation to yourself, and simply go on acting in the way you usually do. This step is difficult, as others believe that you can influence him. You may have been given the opposite suggestion from friends or from other professionals. They are unaware of your abuser's intentions, and may have some respect for him. They may believe that he has honourable intentions, and that he is a responsible partner and father. They might be trained to believe that all problems can be solved by communication. What they are unaware of is that your abuser does not want to find a solution: even when he seems to agree to one today, he will soon be dissatisfied about the solution, or about some other issue.

He keeps you in his game by talking to you

Your abuser does not want the game to end; he wants to keep you on your guard, and he has a well-stocked store of fresh tactics that he can call on when he needs to. Having you as a captive audience for his thoughts and opinions gives him a sense of mastery. Knowing that he can get inside your emotional protection is a source of pride for him on a job well done. Believing that he has colonised and broken your spirit convinces him that he has achieved what he was entitled to achieve. Allowing him to remain convinced of his achievements can be a very useful way to avoid hearing him any more. You may even pretend to agree with him, as this might lessen the tension in your home.

You have heard enough

As you are drawn deeper into his web of lies, deceit, criticism, entitlement and arrogance, you may come to realise that you seldom hear anything from your abuser that soothes you or brings you peace. You may come to recognise that he has no interest in your well-being and is only interested in having you pay attention to him. Listening to him and his selfish talk has kept you on his tread-mill, where he adjusts the speed until you find that you cannot make progress. His ability to make you feel afraid of him has resulted in your increased efforts, until all your energy is being spent in staying upright. He knows that if he drains you of your energy, you will be unlikely to resist his demands. Even when he is not physically present, his voice in your head will demand that you follow his instructions. Your mind is full of his thoughts: you do not need to hear any more of them. The first step in reducing the effect of his voice is not to hear further instructions or threats. This step can be followed without your abuser or others knowing that you no longer heed his threats or his lies.

3. Resist taking the blame
Abuse is not your fault

The initial tactic of every male intimate abuser is to convince you that it is your own fault that you are miserable. You have been blamed for all the tension between you since you first met your abuser. You have also been blamed for his abusive behaviour from an early stage in your relationship. As this tactic developed, you have also begun to blame yourself for the distress and anguish that you are suffering. This deliberate switching of the blame away from your abuser and on to you will initially be accompanied by his attempts to blame outside forces, such as his job, his short fuse, his reaction to alcohol, his unruly children, his lack of social outlets, the way in which he was treated as a young boy in school, and his difficult upbringing. He has learned over time that you may accept one or more of these explanations as excuses for his bad behaviour. He may also have learned that you can feel sorry for him and forgive him, because you believe that his bad behaviour is not his own choice.

Once you remove responsibility from him, you will burden yourself with extra efforts to keep the peace. If you have been seduced into believing that he is only aggressive when he is under the influence of alcohol, you may try to control his drinking. When he drinks too much and behaves aggressively, he will probably blame you for not minding him, or worse, he may tell you that you are the cause of his drinking. If he behaves in an intimidating way towards your children, he may blame you for their lack of respect, or condemn you for their waywardness and lack of success. If your home is dilapidated, he will label you as lazy, even though he refuses to spend money or time on its upkeep. If money is scarce, he may let the whole world know that you are a spendthrift, or he may accuse you of robbing him. If your shared sex life is poor, he will label you as naive or frigid, or maybe even ugly. If he knows how much importance you place on loyalty in marriage, he may accuse you of flirting, or even of having an affair.

He may invite others to side with him, and they may all conspire to persuade you that you are being unreasonable. He is better at grooming than you, and he will find it easy to involve both family and friends who want your relationship to survive, and want to avoid the breakdown of your family life.

Examining your own behaviour takes the focus off him

All of these tactics are very effective in getting you to focus on your own behaviour. Instead of saying that the abuse and violence is his fault, you will spend most of your energy trying to anticipate the next outburst, and judging your own behaviour when he raises the tension. You will convince yourself that you can improve your own performance, and that you will eventually be good enough for him. All the energy that you have spent in trying to meet his standards has probably gone unnoticed, and has definitely been unappreciated. This lack of appreciation is sometimes hidden by the way he gives you presents or treats that you do not really want. But you are seldom asked what you would like, and even his most sincere promises are easily forgotten.

You have been trained to examine yourself against his standards, without knowing how high his standards are. You may be exceptional at housekeeping, only to have him locate dust on some unused surface. You may try to cook a type of food he likes, or time his meals to suit him, only to find your cooking skills being criticised or your timing ignored. You may leave a door open, and be verbally abused for not giving him some privacy, or you may close the same door, and be accused of talking about him behind his back.

He is brilliant at avoiding criticism: you probably find that if you risk trying to explain to him what he is doing wrong, you end up being drawn into his excuse and may regret ever having raised the issue. He can twist even the most simple of your ideas, and convince you that the issue is more complicated than it is and that you do not understand the issue as well as he does. You may even believe that you are unable to properly explain yourself, and take the blame for the breakdown in communications you. You may feel that if you had a better command of language, or if you could form your ideas in a more simple way, you might be able to get through to him. It is possible that you may begin to shout, or even scream, in the belief that all other methods have failed. If you have been living with him for a long time, you may be getting to the stage where you do not trust your own memory, and blame yourself for not being able to match his level of recall.

You may spend hours trying to think of ways to improve your performance in the relationship. You may lie awake at night trying to tell yourself that you are inadequate, and that you are to blame for his bad behaviour, and for the anxiety and fear that dwell in your heart. You may look at other women and tell yourself that you are not as good as they are. You may watch the partners of other women and conclude that your partner is no worse than some other men. If you continue to practise this intimate blame-taking, you will isolate yourself from your friends and family, and eventually become withdrawn from the real world, and exist in the world that he has arranged for you. This world is his prison for you, and you have entered into it without knowing what it is. While you were concentrating on your efforts to improve your performance, he was invading your spirit and strengthening the walls of your emotional prison.

Try not to criticise yourself

Most of my clients want me to understand and accept that the abuse is at least partly their own fault. They present themselves as naive, stupid, over-sensitive or inadequate. You may have already told friends that you do not know how to please him. You may have admitted that you do not really understand him. You may even have convinced yourself that he would be better off with some other woman, and that it would be better for everyone if you were out of his life. You have probably spent sleepless nights debating with yourself whether you are ever going to be good enough. You are likely to have huge feelings of guilt because you believe that you are not good enough, and that the role of any woman is to be able to diminish the tension in her relationship. You may have heard your spouse plead that all he wants is some peace, and that it is your actions that have denied him this peace. He is constantly drawing your attention to your role in the distress, and resisting any attempt you might make to focus on his behaviour. You may have tried repeatedly to get him to recognise the role he plays in increasing the tension between you, but he will seldom if ever examine his own behaviour in this regard.

Focus on him

If you can realise that there is nothing you can do to influence his behaviour, and that the anxiety, confusion, rejection and degradation that you feel has been deliberately created by him, you may begin to put the blame for the abuse on his shoulders. If you begin to focus on his pattern of behaviour, you may find that your abuser seldom takes responsibility for any negative outcomes. He may boast about his achievements or revel in his successes, but he is an expert at avoiding taking the blame for any failure. If you have children, he may criticise them if they are not top of the class or on the first team, but he will invade their graduations and their awards ceremonies as though their successes were all down to his parenting.

He is likely to make himself the centre of public attention when you or your children cannot ignore him. First Communions, Confirmations, Bar Mitzvahs, graduations and weddings are all public occasions where he will present himself as the parent who has provided education and resources to ensure that his children achieve success. He may even publicly acknowledge that he could not have done it without your help. But his presence will take away from your enjoyment of the day, and you will spend much of your energy in alleviating any tension, which might spoil the occasion.

Every psychephile wants to be the centre of his little universe. If he can enhance his image and improve his status, he will do so – by any means. Sometimes he can do so in the wake of some success, but he can also achieve this in the midst of failure. He may prefer to generate some failure, because he finds it easier to exonerate himself, and to transfer the blame to you. His determination to make your life miserable knows no limits, and he will say and do outrageous things just to watch you suffer. He knows your vulnerabilities, and can aim his interventions directly into your heart. He has dismantled your normal emotional shield, and can access and manipulate your emotions at will. If you have shared your inner life with him, he can deny that he has acted in a manipulative way, and tell you that you are the problem. He seems to ignore your distress, but he monitors and stores away the outcome of any of his tactics.

When you feel angry or sad, confused or embarrassed, despairing or hopeless, he has deliberately engendered those feelings. He uses his intimate knowledge of your inner life to achieve whatever effect he is aiming for. His cunning and lies will allow him to hide his responsibility for the upset and to transfer the blame on to you. He is to blame for the abuse, and your reaction will never stop him from carrying out further abuse. He can predict your reaction to his behaviour, and has already decided on the conclusion before he begins to behave badly. He measures the outcome of any negative behaviour by its effect on you, and by his ability to avoid any punitive consequences for himself.

4. Resist being drawn into his way of thinking
You are already immersed in his way of thinking

In the daily flow of your relationship, you will encounter many situations where you are constantly responding in ways that he has decided. If you have been subject to intimate abuse from a male partner for a number of years, you will already be invaded by his way of thinking. You will know intuitively how he views the world, and how he is likely to react in any situation. You will carry his thoughts in your head, and measure your own ideas against his opinions. I describe your position as like being drawn into a swamp, where you cannot find your feet and where your efforts to escape allow him to suck you deeper into the mire.

His demands are never met

It may be useful to begin the process of behaving in ways that suit you and not him. Strangely, this might mean that you continue to act as before, and that outwardly you are behaving as he would wish. But in fact, you are beginning to change your thinking: instead of telling yourself that you are doing what he wants you to do, you begin to remind yourself that you are doing what *you* want to do. This change in your thought-process may already be present, and you may already be acting in the belief that your decisions are in your own best interests. Doing things for your own benefit changes the dynamic of his control, and allows you to examine your decisions differently. When you act in a way that you decide is to your own benefit, you can measure the outcome in terms of the effect it has for you, instead of hearing some criticism from him. Changing the purpose of your action from one of trying to please him to one of pleasing yourself, may help you to avoid efforts you might have made previously to earn his acknowledgement or appreciation. It may seem provocative that you should keep cooking his meals, doing his washing, and sharing a bed where he hurts you – and to do it for your own benefit. What I am tentatively saying is that when you do these things to please him and gain his approval, you are on the endless treadmill of abuse. Changing your motivation to one where you do some things to please yourself will be more rewarding for you.

When you are trying to please him, your efforts draw you into his way of thinking and encourage you to try harder to win his approval – which you will, sadly, never get, since this is not his end goal. Cooking his meals, doing his washing, sharing his bed can all be done because you want to do them for your own safety. Through that shift in perspective, you stand up for yourself, and this will support your self-esteem. Making your life less tense is a valuable goal, and complying with his goals can be of value if you measure your efforts in how you are benefiting in your own life. As you lie in bed at night, you can begin to acknowledge that, by pleasing yourself, you are beginning to regain some small measure of satisfaction in your life. You may also find that your hope is expanding, and that you are very capable of changing your thinking without anyone noticing. You may also start to feel that you are no longer on the uphill struggle that he generates through his demands. There will come a day when you feel psychologically free and safe, and at that point it is entirely up to you if you want to keep up the life you have today, or if you want to make your partner wash his own clothes, or if you want to leave him. I will not tell you what to do, but I want to encourage you to walk the path towards the place where you make your own choices.

There is no acknowledgement of your effort

You may also begin to recognise for yourself that his way of thinking is not the real problem. What is really at issue here is not his level of satisfaction, but the fact that he is never satisfied. This complete lack of recognition or appreciation is part of his game. When he can engage with you in ways that are familiar to him, he will know what he wants to achieve, and he will leave you feeling ignored, and your efforts unrewarded. If you are playing his game, you are listening to his complaints, and adding to your own **self**-criticism. You are on a never-ending treadmill that seldom slows down, and may even go faster when it suits him. He can keep you on the treadmill even when he is not present, and he can influence your decisions and efforts from afar.

He can change his conversation to maintain your confusion

He will have convinced you of his superior knowledge and his selfish entitlement. He will be unlikely ever to accept your ideas, especially if they affect him negatively. Before you can deal with his long-term brainwashing, it is helpful to shut out any more of his ideas. This is an essential step in unravelling the effects of his brainwashing techniques. If he continues to have access to your thoughts, he can keep you groomed into acting in ways that suit him. He can challenge any new ideas that you may be considering. He can threaten punishing reactions to any changes in your behaviour, and he can undermine any progress that he sees you making. He can pull you back if he thinks you are taking any steps to leave his control. All the good suggestions or therapy that you may act on, can be undermined by him in an instant. He will denigrate your supports and tell you that you need him. He will repeat the untruth that all children need a father, and he may threaten you with financial ruin or with child-care intervention by social services. He may suggest that, if he seriously injures or kills himself or others, he will do so in a way that will make you feel guilty. He may state as fact that your friends and family will hold you accountable, and that you will end up alone. While he continues to have access to your spirit, he will intensify his efforts to destroy it.

It is not easy to switch off from this stream of abuse and intimidation, but it might help to keep reminding yourself that his intention is to degrade your humanity and to turn you into an object, which he possesses. He has done a great deal of damage already: being available for more of this negative treatment is unhealthy for your mind and spirit. He is convinced that he owns you, and that you are a lesser human being than he is. He will have already established that his ownership of you extends to your bedroom, and that you are obliged to serve his sexual needs. He has delivered this message by hints and suggestions that diminish your sexual integrity, and he will remind you of his entitlement if you ever dare to negotiate with him.

Change tactics

One of the suggestions that I would cautiously make is that, instead of trying to protect yourself from his conversations, you might begin to agree with him. Telling him that you have come to realise that he was probably right from the beginning, may be a huge untruth, but it will make him feel very successful. Reassuring him that you no longer wish to fight with him, may help reduce the level of tension in your life. While agreeing with him, you may also begin to excuse yourself by admitting to confusion or forgetfulness. You may begin to test the actions you need to carry out in order to keep yourself safe, and you may begin to explore what actions you can get away with. Though you might not like to engage in deceit, as he does, you may console yourself with the realisation that your tactics are designed to protect you and your children from further abuse, whereas his tactics are designed to destroy your spirit. If you are a bad liar, or if you feel that this approach would make you feel more controlled, this suggestion may not be helpful for you.

Stay alert

I need to repeatedly draw your attention to the danger in any change in your behaviour, no matter how small it appears to be. If you initiate any new behaviour, you will need to be satisfied that this is what you want to do. You will also need to avoid alerting or threatening him about any change, as this may result in some risk for you. You will know by now that your abuser can overreact to any small change in your behaviour if he sees it as a threat to his control.

81

5. Stop trying to improve him

His initial good behaviour was an act

Because your abuser presented himself as respectful and caring when you first met him, you may still be trying to make a decent man of him. You may remember how attractive he was, and how he portrayed himself as desirable to you. He may have convinced you that he is still trying to be decent, and that he continues to promise that he is doing his best. He may be able to persuade you that if you make a greater effort, you will be pleased with his behaviour. He may even want you to be sorry for him, and he will want you to forgive him. In some cases, you may still get a glimpse of the man you fell in love with, so that your hope will be renewed and your efforts to improve your relationship will be increased. He will try to expand your hope, while you struggle to be convinced that he is genuine. He may even resort to telling your friends and family what a wonderful wife and mother you are, so that the people who know you both will want you to keep the relationship intact. This is a charade which is designed to seduce you and to cover his malevolent intentions.

Do not become his mother

You may have tried to get help from others in an attempt to improve him, or to learn how to survive in the relationship until he goes back to being the attractive man you fell in love with. As a kind and committed woman, you may have rejected any thought of giving up on him, and you may even have prayed that he would behave honourably towards you and your children. You may compare your abuser to a big child, one who throws a tantrum unless he gets what he wants. Your hope is that he will eventually grow up to be an adult. This hope invites you to take on the role of mother to your psychephile, and you will make many attempts to anticipate his mistakes and cover up for his failures. Like most mothers, you blame yourself if he does not improve, and it suits him to let you take the blame. If you, as a mother, take the blame for the misbehaviour of your child, you may rear a spoiled and arrogant adult who does not take responsibility for the hurt they might cause to others. But your child may eventually change, and choose to behave responsibly, whereas your adult partner will grow more entrenched in his arrogance and his entitlement. By increasing your efforts to make a decent man out of him, you will set yourself up for being dismissed as a nagging wife who is impossible to please.

He does not allow you to guide him

Unfortunately, he is never going to be good for you, and all his acting and his promises were only designed to deceive you into beginning a relationship with him. He is in reality a selfish, arrogant and entitled man who sees nothing wrong in controlling you. It is possible that he is incapable of growing up, and that he will go through life believing that the world owes him a lot, even if he does little to earn it. He may appear to be a good father or a good partner in public, as this supports his vanity, but in the confines of his home, he controls anything that might diminish his power. He does this deliberately: although you might imagine him as a big child who cannot control his outbursts, it is chilling to realise that he is always in control of his outbursts, and is aware of the outcome of any tantrum before he starts it. He will ignore your pleadings and your efforts to educate him into being a constructive father and lover. An abusive man has no intention of fulfilling these roles, and he will only ignore the pleadings of his family. He may groom some of his children to collude with him in controlling you. It is much more honest for you to admit that he does not pay any attention to your suggestions, and that his arrogance, and his skill in lying, make it impossible for you to have any influence over him.

I give my clients permission to resign from the positions of mother and slave, and to realise that they may never have had a position of equality in the relationship. The sadness is in the realisation that he never loved you, but loved what you did for him. It may bring agony to your life if you realise that your efforts are in vain, and that your dedication and forgiveness were never appreciated. The other side of the coin is that you may now also realise that you no longer have to be worn down by trying to do the impossible. You are allowed to redirect your kindness, compassion and willingness to see the value in every person, on to yourself, so that you too can benefit from the wonderful person that you are.

Resist making excuses or granting forgiveness

You may see your abuser as a man who has had a poor upbringing, and that the abuse you suffer is a result of the neglect or abuse that he suffered. You may see his anger as a consequence of his experience of the anger of others. You may believe that the fear he generates in you is his way of avoiding the fear of being helpless. These excuses are the ones that he would want you to accept: in doing so, you will transfer your criticism away from him and onto the bad people in his life. Many of my clients have had a similarly difficult life, and are respectful partners. You may be one of these women: you will instinctively know that past history is no excuse for abusive behaviour.

He may also invite you to understand him, and have you believe that once you acknowledge his excuses, you will get a clearer picture of what is happening, and the reasons why he behaves badly. This effort to understand him is doomed, because he never reveals his true self to you. Though you may share his bed for years and rear his children, you will come to realise that you do not know him at all. He will remain a mystery to you, because there is a huge gap between his words and his actions.

Your own principles will encourage you to forgive your partner repeatedly. I would like you to remember that forgiveness is wasted on anyone who is not sorry, and is definitely of no value for someone who is convinced he did nothing wrong. Forgiving someone who is sorry for the harm he caused – instead of being sorry so that he will not suffer any consequence – is always worthwhile, but repeated forgiveness for someone who does not appreciate it, is detrimental. He will grow more entitled, and his sense of arrogance will expand.

Summary

Awareness

Keep your thoughts to yourself.

- Information about you feeds his store of ammunition.
- He uses several sources for this information

Stop listening to his message.

- He uses words to establish his terms and conditions.
- He uses words to groom and re-groom you.

Resist taking the blame.

- Taking the blame has meant that you examine your own behaviour. Taking the blame means that you ignore or excuse his behaviour.

Resist being drawn into his thinking.

- He justifies and enforces his opinions with lies.
- He rejects your honesty and dismisses your instincts.

Stop trying to improve him.

- He regards you as second-class, so you have no right to influence him.
- He does not want to improve.

Chapter Seven

Steps 6 to 11: Confirmation

6. Examine his behaviour for intention and effect

He is clever

One of the alarming and confusing things that I have learned about all psyche-philes is how clever and capable they are. Your abuser may be highly educated or he may have finished his schooling early in life, but he will have an innate cunning that is difficult to define. He may have a profound knowledge of behavioural psychology without ever having read a book on the subject. He will have an ability to be devious, which he practises and develops until he is as good as any self-serving politician or unscrupulous banker. He might try to hide behind his naivety when he is exposed, but he will reinvent himself as an expert as soon as he is back in control. His instinct and ready intuition are talents which are applied to a very limited and focused aim. He is alert to every opportunity to degrade you and to enhance his own position. The speed with which he operates can create a doubt in your mind as to whether something really happened. His ability to redirect any discussion into one of blame and criticism can leave you feeling stupid for having raised the issue. He can create doubt and confusion in your thoughts while claiming to be reasonable. He can twist the conversation without you knowing it, so that, having tried to be reasonable or helpful, you end up feeling frustrated or even frightened.

You will probably have got to the stage where you have said to yourself that there is no point in talking to him, but you nonetheless get drawn back into the same old discussions, which you know you can never win. It might be the case that instead of being angry with him for his manipulative approach, you are angry with yourself for being such a fool. Use the energy of this anger to tell yourself 'no' when your mind seeks to blame yourself. I hope that, like some of my clients, bit by bit you will regain your ability to know where your responsibility ends and his starts. Practise, in the privacy of your mind, refusing to take all the blame, and putting blame on him instead. Don't confront him, and don't do this to everyone around you until you have gained a safe sense of what a normal balance of responsibility between partners should feel like.

He knows what he is doing to you

This confusion, and the possibility of you being angry with yourself, is part of the hidden purpose of all his conversations. In the intimacy of your relationship you will have revealed your confusion, and you may have admitted to your frustration and anger. He is really pleased to be reassured by you that his tactics are working and that he is undermining your own thinking process. He listens to you when you tell him of your anxiety, your embarrassment and your fear. He appears not to be listening because his response is not to soothe you but to expand the distress that you feel. This is why you are convinced that he never listens to you.

Any human relationship that has a value will develop a process where each partner can at least show recognition of the distress that the other is feeling. A psychephile will not do this, but will store the information and explore ways to increase the negative impact of his conversation. He may appear decent to the rest of the world, and you may feel unable to pinpoint or explain to others what you can deeply sense as true malevolence, or even evil. Others may say that evil does not exist. This is an ongoing debate between my colleagues and me, one we have settled by saying that science has not yet explained the origins of the degrading, persistent and extremely harmful behaviours of the intimate abuser. Until that happens, I want to recognise and respect your experience of being put through evil; if society tells you that you overreact or are too sensitive, they should count themselves lucky that they haven't experienced anything similar to what you have been through. When my colleagues and I worked with groups of male intimate abusers, we experienced a sense of malevolence that exceeded that among groups of child abusers.

He monitors your reaction and that of others

While your partner may not be a psychologist, he develops a clear and accurate picture of your thinking patterns and uses your own thoughts to expand your anxieties and to orchestrate your fears. This psychological expertise is developed by his instinctive evaluation of the information he needs to collect, and by his monitoring of its usefulness in any conversation. His evaluation and decision is not cluttered by noise in the form of concern for you. This results in his ability to generate any reaction he wants from you. His unending monitoring of the depth of that impact will allow him to develop a range of powerful tactics through which he will be able to generate any effect he wants for you, in a precise and accurate way. You may already be aware of how your partner tries to control other parts of his life. You may have listened to his explanations and efforts at getting his own way. You may have witnessed how he reacts with his work colleagues and how he works very hard at getting what he wants at work. You may also be aware that he suits himself when it comes to his own family of origin, and that even his acts of kindness are designed to enhance his image with his parents or his siblings. Or he may have already given up on his own family because they have recognised his selfishness.

Your loyalty and helpfulness is used as a mean of coercion because you do not get appreciation and results from showing it, but punishment and blame when you deviate from being kind and loyal. This skewed, almost invisible pattern of coercion pushes you into a corner, where you see no other way out of it than being more loyal and more helpful. This twisted kind of feedback is very hard to detect in each particular moment. Keep noticing what his feedback makes you feel, not what it makes you do.

You may even be aware of how he grooms your children. He may treat them all with disrespect while demanding respect from them. He may try to terrorise them with threats and intimidation or win them over with rewards and gifts. He may single out some of his children for special status and condemn others to criticism and abuse. In every relationship that matters to him, he practises his controlling tactics and monitors the success or failure of each tactic.

He learns what he needs to know

Your controlling partner is like every other psychephile in an intimate relationship, setting out to establish sexual dominance and priority over his partner. Every seductive or abusive behaviour is designed for his benefit. While he may appear to be switched off to your pleadings, he monitors and stores your reactions to his various tactics. When he speaks to you or acts towards you in a particular way, he already knows how you will be affected, or he may be trying something out, in order to gauge your reaction. As his skill develops and his knowledge of your thinking expands, he can accurately predict the outcome of any engagement with you. He can make you angry or sad, anxious or confused, compliant or frightened, by deliberately picking a topic that will work.

He knows which one to choose because you have told him repeatedly what effect any particular tactic has on you. He is also aware, before he starts any discussion, that he can achieve any outcome he wishes, by manipulating your emotions. He knows the amount of effort needed to help him avoid sanction, because he has learned how to re-groom you. His intention is to get what he wants at as little cost as possible to himself. This level of information about you and your spirit is unique to an adult intimate relationship: he probably knows more about you than anyone else in your world. You may even begin to believe that he knows you better than you know yourself. This sensation is a result of your decreasing space to move – you do fewer and more predictable things – and the way you are unable to sense his greater agenda of controlling you. It's no surprise that he has so much knowledge of you: it is the result of diligent work on his part.

He achieves sexual priority

The sexual control that each psychephile achieves can vary in both intensity and practice. The most common form of sexual behaviour for a psychephile is one of frequency and immediacy. If you are in relationship with one of these men, you will probably have been obliged to engage in sexual behaviour when he demands it. You may feel that it is the right thing to do because you believe that being intimate with him will earn you some respect, and you may experience some pleasure. But your partner is only interested in his own pleasure and is unconcerned about your satisfaction. He believes that your role is to bring him pleasure or relief, and that he is entitled to this 'service' whenever he wants it. This man seldom acts with restraint, and carries the belief that your role is to offer him implied consent which does not need to be renewed. In his mind, you have already said yes, and he does not need to ask again. The frequency of your sexual encounters is dictated by him, and if you do not comply, he might force you into intimacy or he might become involved with another woman. The frequency may be dictated by his energy or his age, and as he gets older he may tend to ignore you.

He hides his unacceptable sexual needs

The psychephile in your life may be different than the norm. He may be a man who is regularly unfaithful and is not demanding towards you because he has other sources of pleasure and relief. He might be bisexual or gay but does not want to be exposed. Some men are impotent and use the relationship to conceal their sexual embarrassment. He may express distress – fake or honest – over his inadequacy. You might feel honoured and trusted at first, because you have been chosen to help this man you love. Your love and trust for him might increase when you find him sensitive and well tuned-in to his more 'fragile' sides. In the guise of him needing your support to feel adequate, he may slowly increase the demands on you. He may eventually say that he can only get pleasure from hurting you, or from watching heavy porn with you, or photographing you to show his friends. In case this happened to you, be aware that you are not the only one this happened to, and you are not to blame for this abuse of your integrity and willingness to help. If you are at a point with a partner where he is using this kind of verbal coercion, please take notice and think twice if you can accept my point of view that a truly sensitive, emotionally well tuned-in person simply does not use their partner in this kind of way. In all of these cases, I hope it is a great relief to you if you locate the problem accurately and recognise that you are not the frigid, naive or inadequate partner that you have been labelled as by your abuser.

He expects to be successful

While your partner can be seen as clever or even cunning, he is stupid enough to believe that he will break your spirit. He is also foolish enough to miss the reality of a loving relationship, where he could have his needs met in a caring and healthy way. He does not know that you may still have a place for him in your heart, and that your kindness and loyalty are not completely gone. He ignores you when you plead with him to treat you with the dignity that any person deserves. You may have got to a place where you would settle for some peace even if your relationship was dead. If he hears you express such thoughts, he is delighted that he has broken your spirit and shattered your dreams. He is satisfied that your thoughts are transparent and that he can invade your spirit. He is indifferent to the cost to you and your children. He is deliberate in his clever use of tactics that maintain your distress but keep you available to him. You may be one of many women who find this behaviour unbelievable, and even the survivors of these behaviours find it hard to explain them. I think the best word I have to describe his behaviour is 'evil'; you should acknowledge the great strength you have shown to have remained sane while living with such a man. You may feel defeated but I remind you again that there is a part of you which is not damaged but hidden: it is not gone.

7. Accept that his behaviour is deliberate

He is always in control

One of the scary aspects of the behaviour of an intimate abuser is that he does nothing by chance. While he will claim that he did not intend to be hurtful, or that he cannot remember being abusive, the reality is that he can 'switch on' and manage the abuse whenever he wishes. He may look and sound angry, and may blame alcohol or drugs, but he is still in charge of his actions, and can measure his behaviour in terms of desired outcomes. His abusive and criminal behaviour is designed to maintain control of the level and type of sexual activity in the relationship. If you are a reasonable and decent person, it will be difficult for you to imagine that any person would deliberately inflict this level of distress on the person that wants to love him. You may be very slow to recognise that much of what he tells you is exaggerated or untrue.

Because you take people at face value and act truthfully most of the time, it is hard for you to acknowledge that his lies are not accidental or careless, but are specifically designed to confuse your thinking and to enhance his position. He is devious and calculating in many parts of his life. He is cunning, skilled and very manipulative, while appearing to be responsible and reasonable. As I have already mentioned, he does not engage in any conversation or argument without being confident of knowing the outcome in advance. He has gained this knowledge because of the unique intimate context in which he operates, and because you have repeatedly conceded to him in previous discussions. He also knows that he can make you confused, anxious, embarrassed, angry or frightened whenever he chooses. He knows this because you have told him repeatedly about the effect he has on you. He likes to know that he can push the right button and create the desired reaction in your mind. He has monitored his developing skill in dictating your emotional life and he feels reassured every time you tell him that he has been successful.

He feeds on your response

When you plead with him to stop upsetting you, he hears your request as a further acknowledgement of his influence over you. He deliberately wants to have direct access to your emotional life and to be able to manipulate your feelings in whatever way suits him. By dismantling your emotional protection, he can instantly change your feelings. It may be difficult for you to admit, but a change in his facial expression or a variation in his tone of voice can have a profound effect on your psyche. The idea that this is all done deliberately is hard to accept and difficult to explain. He is thrilled when others tell you that he did not mean to upset you. Though you may not know how he operates, you can begin to tell yourself that however you end up feeling was exactly what he planned before he started. If he wants you to be happy or sad, he can do so instantly, and he can change your mood from one to the other effortlessly. He has deliberately destroyed your emotional defences so that he can invade your inner world when it suits him. The only times his actions are truly ambiguous, is when he is unsure of your current state of mind. Instead of forcing himself into your thinking through threats or intimidation, he might send out various messages to find out which triggers you react to. This is not a change of conviction or perspective on his part: it is all a way to get enough of a response from you to know that he is still in control of your mind.

He is not always abusive

If there is no resistance to his demands, he can be non-abusive. The psychephile is not addicted to his behaviours. He does not get a buzz from beating or raping you. What excites him is the godlike feeling of owning another person and being able to do what he wishes with you. What really appeals to him is the successful way he can be in charge of the level and type of sexual activity between you. All the other controlling tactics are geared to undermine your resistance to his sexual agenda. Your abuser may be demanding and may try to convince you that if you respond actively, you will be rewarded with a more peaceful relationship. He may be unfaithful, but will blame his betrayal on your sexual reticence. He may have a sexual deviance or he may be gay, but he will blame you for your sexual frustration. He may reject your sexual advances or refuse you affection when you seek it. When you comply with his suggestions, he may be calm and non-abusive, and he may continue in that mode until you try to renegotiate with him or refuse him.

He may have no conscience or may ignore it when he is with you

Many therapists believe that your abuser develops a conscience and tries to make amends for the harm he has done, and to repair or even strengthen your relationship. This is a fallacy: there is no honeymoon period in an abusive relationship. Your partner does not believe that he has done anything wrong, or that you deserve any compensation or kinder treatment, because he believes that it is your fault that he behaved in the way he did. He might make a public display of recompense which impresses others, but if he truly intended to make amends, he would listen to your wishes and provide you with something that would be of value to you. Instead, he knows that by appearing to be contrite, he limits your ability to be angry with him, and he can describe you as ungrateful if you do not respond appreciatively to his efforts.

You may not be able to recall if he ever asked you what you would like; even if he did, it is unlikely that he complied with your request. You may be like many clients who describe the charade that he engages in after an abusive episode as being more hurtful than the event itself. This may be because, while you excuse his bad behaviour, you know that the creepy feeling you get when he 'acts nice' to you is an accurate indication that you are being manipulated and that you are helpless to stop it. Take note of the creepy feeling: it is your guide to learning that you are being manipulated.

He chooses when and how to act

If he has no conscience when it comes to his relationship with you, it means that he has no buffer which might limit the damage that he can do to you. What might limit the harm that he does is his realisation either that he can control you with a limited amount of intimidation, or that his malevolence may be exposed to the community. His concern for his image might be what is keeping you alive. This is yet another reason for you to stay observing and cautious, and not make any changes until you are relatively safer and clear-headed. Rushing to act in a new way or confronting your partner can compromise your safety.

It might be better for you to recognise that the length of time between abusive episodes is not dependent on his false remorse, but on his ability to generate compliance in your behaviour and forgiveness in your attitude. If you continue to express your dissatisfaction or anxiety, if you decline to be influenced by his attempts to control you, it is inevitable that his remorse will disappear and his abusive behaviour will be renewed. You will probably remember various times in your relationship when the level of tension was low and you felt somewhat content. When that happened, you might have thought that he was making an effort to improve, and that he was becoming more respectful. These times are deliberately designed to give you false hope, or they may have been periods when he felt unchallenged. Looking back, you may notice that when the tension came back into your relationship, you were blamed for causing the change. He did this so that you would feel guilty for disturbing the harmony between you. You may also notice that when the tension was low, you continued to feel that you had to be careful and alert, so that he would remain calm. It is unlikely that you breached any of the initial 'terms and conditions' of the relationship without him quickly condemning you for your carelessness. A change from calm may come from frustrations in his outside world that have triggered his need for dominance over you, or from him not feeling in control over you.

Admitting that his behaviour is deliberate is a powerful step in recognising that you have no role to play in his behaviour. His intention is to suit himself, and his methods do not allow him to acknowledge the cost to others. You can recognise his aims if you notice the feelings that he generates in you. Your confusion, frustration, anger and fear are all deliberately put there by him. Many targets of abuse say that something felt odd or wrong from the start, but that they did not listen. If this is true for you, let go of any self-blaming or regret. We humans are primed to take on challenges when our well-being or possessions are in danger of disappearing. We are supposed to problem-solve, to evaluate the bad of something against possible explanations for this bad. We have been successful as a species by being able to put the greater good of the group ahead of momentary good for ourselves. In short, we are primed to act against our personal short-term benefit and that is what I believe you are doing when you give your new partner the benefit of the doubt.

Try to look ahead. If you encounter the same feeling of something odd when your partner acts in the future, heed that possible warning to see if this is yet another way of manipulating you. Try not to rush you into doing the same things again. Remember that, first of all, you should strive only to notice these emotions and thoughts, without acting on them. Do what you have always done until you feel safe enough to try to act differently. Always keep your immediate safety first. Never confront the abusive person with your observations if you do not feel absolutely safe to do so. Never confront your partner to make him change. He might change, but in a way that is even more damaging and controlling to you. Stay safe by keeping your observations to yourself, and act differently only when you feel safe to do so.

8. Observe his re-grooming
He can get you to forgive and forget

Your abuser is constantly operating in ways that mean you will return to serving him without noticing the cost to you. If he feels any resistance, he will increase or vary his tactics until you become compliant. As you begin to rethink your relationship, you will notice that you have little or no say in how the relationship is renewed. He will seldom ask you what you think should be done to resolve the abuse, but instead will insist that he has the answer to your problem. On reflection, you may begin to realise that not only does he commit the abuse, but he also supplies the explanation while monitoring your response to his tactics. He knows how to intimidate you, how to frighten you, how to terrify you, and how to seduce you. He becomes skilled at getting you to forget his behaviour, and to return to the relationship as though nothing had happened. He will demand that you move on, and deny you an opportunity to discuss the latest scar on your spirit.

Re-grooming is a development of the initial grooming

What he is doing is developing and repeating the tactics which he has found to be most useful since he first met you. He develops these tactics by monitoring their effects and by listening to your reactions. While you are immersed in the daily routine of anticipation and anxiety, it is difficult to recognise and resist the subtle tactics that he uses to keep you controlled. You have come to expect,

Don Hennessy

and maybe accept, his re-grooming as part of his reasonable attempts to move on from his bad behaviour. He may even have convinced you that, as he has already moved on from the most recent abuse, it is unfair of you to bring it up in conversation. He will want you to believe that his behaviour is normal and that you are being over-sensitive. He may try to convince you that he did not mean to be hurtful, and that he is just repeating the pattern of his parents' relationship. If he thinks that it is useful, he may apologise to you and promise you that he will do better in the future.

Your intuition will be upset

You may observe these tactics and try to believe his good intentions, but you will probably have an uneasy feeling about what he does and says. Over time, you may have told yourself that you know that he is lying to you, or that he does not keep his promises. You may also realise that even when he appears to be nice to you, the conversation leaves you feeling uneasy or angry. It is possible that you give him the benefit of any doubt that you have, and instead of saying that he is acting deliberately, try to convince yourself that he does not know about your distress. You probably recognise that he seldom if ever makes you feel good about yourself, and that even though he seems to be nice to you, he manages to make you more anxious. It is very difficult to pinpoint how he affects you while you are invaded by his opinions and ideas. He knows that he can wear you down by his vigilance and persistence. Every psychephile knows how to live in your thoughts, and your abuser will ensure that you will not be distracted with your own thoughts, or the recommendations of others.

His range of tactics is deliberately focused on your personality traits, and is designed to allow him to get away with his abuse. He knows how to manipulate you into forgetting your distress and encouraging you to forgive him. He is an expert in keeping you on the treadmill of your relationship and getting you to increase your efforts to live up to the commitments that you have made. These tactics will usually allow him to avoid sanction, and to dictate the follow-up.

He has his own solution

He will not ask you what you would like, but will prescribe an action or gift which will pressure you into forgetting the abuse. He creates the problem and then deliberately designs the solution, so that you will feel obliged to forget the abuse and accept his response. I doubt if he has ever asked you what you would need in order to recover from your suffering, and I am sure that even if you made a specific request, your suggestion has been ignored. You may be living with a false sense of hope, or you may have descended into a level of despair that makes your struggle seem endless and your energy drained. It may

94

be difficult to be clear about how he re-grooms you, but analysing what he wants may lead you to notice what he does to achieve his selfish goals.

9. Admit that his behaviour is beyond belief
Nobody understands him

It is very difficult for most humans to grasp the notion that a man is capable of intentionally focusing on the emotional, sexual and spiritual destruction of someone who is an intimate partner and possibly also the mother of his children. I want to tentatively suggest an explanation to the motivation that drives a man to behave in a way that can be described as evil from its persistent, degrading and harmful effects and the pleasure the abusive partner seems to get from the control. Sooner or later, as we get closer to a person, most people will start defending a fellow human being for almost anything he or she has done. This is true for our friends and family, but also when we judge others. The very ability to take another person's perspective into account – which a majority of people have – seems to be the very thing that makes us comprehend the lack of this concern. Furthermore, most professionals are trained to access the decent side of every person and to expand that decency, so that the good behaviour will eventually outweigh the havoc created by them. Because your abuser is cunning and devious, he knows that he can hide from the most skilful of professionals, and resist any attempts to define his behaviour. He can persuade any person who wishes to help, that his agenda is legitimate and that, together, they can cooperate in improving the life of your family. The abusive man seems equally pre-programmed to see the good, but only in himself.

He is confident that he will avoid diagnosis

This skill allows him to dictate the response of most people, and persuades you to ignore your own anxiety. You will examine your own input, and may conclude that you also do not understand the reality of his lies, and that every effort you have made to explain your position has been misunderstood. This isolation encourages you to question your own sanity and to accept his superior knowledge. You may eventually convince yourself that nobody really knows the reality of your experience, and that it is your inability to explain yourself that causes others to minimise your experience. Your explanations and conversations are not the cause of your isolation. The language and the detail you share with others are not the reason why they fail to accept your interpretation of your relationship. The obstacles that you encounter are caused by the failure of your audience to accept an accurate diagnosis of the man you are living with. This failure is a result of the listener's inability or unwillingness to accept that a man can behave in ways that are difficult to believe. The failure is more pronounced when the listener has already met your abuser and has been subjected to his influence.

When you meet a person who has a position that is different from yours, it is possible for you to suggest that you can agree to disagree when you are not convinced. In your inner world, however, you would feel that your core beliefs are unchanged and would feel that this was justified, albeit a bit awkward, perhaps. The abuser does the same. It is easy for him to do. What is invisible and incomprehensible is the core belief of the abusive man: he is 100 percent entitled to his opinion, and there is nothing that will change it. In his ideal world, he has no reason to change. As long as other humans are unable to grasp his behaviour because they are clouded by their own core beliefs of respect and consideration for others, and entitlement only when it is fairly deserved, then this remains an ideal world to him.

You have never told the full story

Another obstacle which creates a barrier that comes between you and your listener is the fact that you will not reveal your total experience of the relationship. Out of a sense of loyalty or shame, you may have experienced events that you will keep secret. You may be reluctant to explain in detail the abuse and degradation you have suffered. This reluctance can be founded on your uncertainty as to the cause of your suffering. You may be convinced that your distress is the result of your own failings, and that other women would tolerate or ignore the emotional rollercoaster that leaves you in pain. You may be convinced that your abuser is not all bad and that, as such, he deserves the sympathy and support that you give to others.

You are entitled to the privacy of your heart and your spirit. There is no need for you to open your soul to people who will not understand you or criticise you, and it is not your job to educate professionals. The failure of the professions is the result of ambivalence and tolerance on their part. Our community, our cultures and our religions are unsure about the equality of the sexes. There is a constant uncertainty about your right to sexual integrity. You are denigrated in your sexual autonomy because of our ambivalence about procreation. In other words, many believe that your role in an intimate relationship is to be available to your partner and to have his children. You are regarded by the community as an autonomous person in some ways but as an object when it comes to sexual activity. Being a sexual object, you are denied the right to protect yourself and you are required to ignore your humanity and be subservient to your abuser.

Social tolerance

You are also expected to tolerate a level of manipulation which is difficult to explain and is acceptable to observers. One radio presenter berated one of his listeners because she was terrified of her boss, who repeatedly threw paperclips at her. The presenter was unable to grasp the cumulative effect of constant small but accurate assaults, and thought that the woman should just put up with her boss's behaviour. This level of tolerance is widespread, and you and other abused women are constantly invited to put up with such behaviour, because it is seen as trivial or not intentionally harmful. Society is unable to grasp the fact that once a power differential is established, every tactic that emphasises this differential is effective, no matter how small.

You are his project

The energy and consistency, the deviousness and manipulation, and the seduction and degradation which the abusive man directs towards you is hard to describe and impossible to quantify. The most unbelievable part of his behaviour is his sense of entitlement, which allows him to remain convinced that his behaviour is not wrong. He eventually combines this behaviour with a feeling of arrogance, which persuades him that he will get away with his crimes. Others may see a man like this as delusional but, viewed through the confusion he has already created, you may believe that he is right. This confusion will be shared by others, even if they found his behaviour delusional at first. As soon as others consider his story, from him or from you, the listener is clouded by their own humane viewpoint. Any person with the more common view point – that we must assume some level of good intent in others – finds that it becomes impossible to keep their original black-and-white insight of how delusional and extreme the abuser's viewpoint is.

His persistence is amazing because he is constantly alert to your behaviour. He can interrupt your social life or he can appear to encourage you to have friends, and then condemn these friends as being no good for you. Every aspect of your life needs to be examined by him, so that his control is secret and his abuse effective. The concentration and the attention that he pays to you and your life would be admirable if it was done for your benefit, but his goals are selfish, and his aim is to de-humanise you. He gives free rein to his cunning and deviousness, and directs all this energy towards you.

Nobody will believe the truth

Because the professionals you encounter, and most of the friends that want to help you, are unable to grasp the reality of his behaviour, it may be time for you to give up on your efforts to get others to believe your reality. Because you are forced into believing that you do not understand him, and that you are naive or stupid, it may be time to stop trying to diagnose him. His ability to hide his true ambition is the foundation of his talents. It seems that what adds to the incomprehensible quality of his behaviours, and the fact that he gets away with them, is that he is exercising a sense of being entitled to a good life, where others respect him and he is in control, to an extent that is beyond belief to most other humans. Anyone who is capable of concern for others, be it mainly learned or genuinely grounded in their personality, cannot fathom someone expecting to be respected and entitled if they have not first deserved to be treated in this way.

You can spare your energy and refocus some of your thinking if you agree that trying to explain him to others is impossible. It is impossible because he remains hidden, and even you, who knows him perhaps better than anyone, are confused about his behaviour and his intentions. By harvesting and protecting your own energy, you will gain some clarity into the deviousness of your abuser, and you may come to realise that his reality is beyond our finite thinking. Like us, you may conclude that the ability of a psychephile to destroy the only person who wants to love him defies belief. It appears as if his sense of self-righteousness gives the abuser a point of view where anything that challenges his power is wrong. That you love him is, in his mind, only what he deserves. If you do anything that challenges his sense that he has a complete claim on your love and devotion, it will be perceived by him as a violation of his absolute rights. Your love is not a gift to him or something he earned by treating you fairly, it is his possession: some abusive men will state clearly that the fact that their partner kept coming back to them is undeniable proof that he is right when he says that he can own her, because she gave herself to him.

You do not need to believe me, but I will be delighted if my suggestions help you clear your thoughts and protect your mental health.

10. Go to counselling that will offer you protection
He does not give you space

Many abused women come to me with a plea to help them cope. It is not possible to cope with mind-control if you are constantly accessible to the controller. Counsellors tend to respond positively to your request, and both you and the counsellor may engage in stages two and three of the recovery process before stage one has been completed.

The first step in counselling is to create a safe space where the client can explore and grow. This exploration will be counterproductive as long as the abuser has access to your thoughts. Many abused women spend years in counselling to help them cope and end up feeling inadequate because, even with professional help, they become less able to cope, and more trapped and despondent. Find someone who can help you to protect your psyche, and when your spirit is safe you can engage in counselling if you wish.

Your therapist may accept your diagnosis

Most counsellors are trained to be non-judgemental. This is an impossible goal for many professionals as they are only human, and come with their own biases and prejudices. Most counsellors also believe in approaching each client with unconditional positive regard. This positive position is undermined by your ability to blame yourself and to explain your distress in terms of your own behaviour. Most counsellors will begin to believe that you have a role to play in your own anxiety and that, by reducing this role, they will be able to help you to develop new coping skills. Your ability to blame yourself was established by him from the beginning of your relationship and has been expanded by him ever since. You may not be aware that you are taking some or all of the blame, and both you and your counsellor may be unaware of his mind-control. Your counsellor may not recognise the skilled brainwashing that you have experienced, and you may be unable to explain it to them.

The psychephile speaks through you

You will probably want to help the counsellor by giving her a picture of your life and the distress that you are experiencing. You will minimise his worst behaviours because you want to be loyal to him. You will exaggerate your own role in the behaviour because you will want the counsellor to see you as not perfect. You will encourage the counsellor to direct some of the blame on to you, and to forgive the psychephile and maybe even to have some pity for him. You will use his language and his descriptions, his explanations and his excuses, in a way that will convince the counsellor that, together, you can anticipate and manage his bad behaviour.

He can influence your therapy without being there

This is the trap that is so appealing to the psychephile. He is happy to know that you and your therapist are talking about him without having any idea of what he has already done. He may even be delighted that he also has power over your therapist, and that he can manipulate your therapy by encouraging you to attend, because you are the one with the problem, or by issuing threats which can invade the safe space that is needed for therapy. Some of my clients were terrified that the man might discover that they were going for therapy. The abuser might express anger initially, and demand that you reveal all the details of your counselling. Once he can put pressure on you to report your conversations with your counsellor, he may even want to speak with your therapist, or he will encourage you to give the counsellor his view of the world.

The psychephile is arrogantly confident that he can undermine the basis for your therapy and can invade the quiet space that you need with your counsellor. He invades that space by arriving into your thoughts and inviting you into a hidden debate between the guidance of your counsellor and his established opinions. Your counsellor may be unaware of this internal conversation and may be critical of your progress. She may be frustrated that you are stuck, and may terminate the sessions because of his influence. Many counsellors that I have met also become afraid of your abuser, and they may wilt, faced with the persistent nature of his behaviour.

You may have spent a long time with one therapist or you may have moved through several forms of therapy, but it is unlikely that your experience in the relationship has changed, or that your despair has diminished. This growth in your desperation is fuelled by the realisation that, even though you are getting professional help, your confidence and hope have not expanded and that you may even feel more inadequate and more despondent. This initial contract between you and the counsellor is designed to improve your life and strengthen your resolve. It is based on the belief that you have an extra store of energy that you can begin to use in ways that will diminish the tension in your life. This initial contract will, however, be built on an incomplete picture of your life and because of that, it will not make matters better. Because of the abuse, your emotions and thoughts are skewed in a way that very few professional people today can examine: because of this lack of an accurate assessment, they may fail to help you. This is not your fault: it is not a result of your inability to explain, or fully understand, your abuser.

The process may become endless

It is also very sad that professionals or well-intentioned friends believe that talking about your problems will make them easier to manage. The reality is that you will not reveal the depth of your anguish or the depravity of his manipulation. You will try to present your problem in a logical and reasonable way, while your real problem presents as beyond both reason and logic. You will hope that you will be understood, even though you really do not understand what is happening, and why. You will pray that the counsellor will believe you, when the truth is that the behaviour of the psychephile is unbelievable. You will arrive at the therapy sessions with a sense of anxiety which will not be completely explored. You will not want a complete diagnosis of the relationship, because you are ashamed of the detail and unsure of your role in it. You may even be convinced that the abuse and suffering are all your own fault, and that the purpose of the therapy is to make you a better person who makes less mistakes. This is a swamp into which you and your counsellor may descend, and in which your delighted partner wants you to stay.

If you instigate any obvious change that makes him unhappy, he will undermine your progress and criticise your counsellor. He is an expert at regaining control, and can do so without you being aware of it. Your sessions may be dominated by your attempts to understand him or by your efforts to get a better understanding of yourself. This agenda suits him, and may leave you wallowing in confusion. This confusion is one of his tactics, as he knows that when you are confused, you are less likely to try anything new. He has already got you to engage in endless discussions with him, either face to face or in the privacy of your own mind. Any new ideas will end up being part of the same conversations, and will go round in circles, without ever coming to an end.

Your therapy sessions may develop the same pattern, and result in the counsellor losing energy or in you dropping out of the work. Several clients of mine have dropped out of previous therapies on more than one occasion, and have become more depressed after each failure. The failure of any therapy that is trying to deal with the behaviour of a psychephile is not due to a lack of professionalism or a lack of honesty but is mainly caused by a complete absence of understanding of the dynamics of abuse, and the abuser. There are very few books that explain the how and the why of the actions of a psychephile. There are numerous books on the application of counselling principles to the target-woman, and some on how to use therapy with the offender. All these interventions are second-phase issues, the first phase being protection for the target and stopping further abuse by the abuser.

Beware of being diagnosed

I have worked with counsellors and therapists all over the country and have heard inexperienced people give various diagnoses of the mental health of victims of intimate abuse. These so-called experts have told me that their clients were withdrawn or angry, naive or devious, depressed or careless, alcoholic or promiscuous, borderline or manic. This process of diagnosis of the victim is a violation of the reality of any woman's life. I hope that neither you nor any other partner of a psychephile is subjected to such an unhelpful assessment, and the subsequent explanations and recommendations. It is inevitable that the guidance you receive will be risky when it comes from a profession that has failed to diagnose your abuser.

Being invited to go to counselling or being referred to therapy implies that the difficulties in your relationship are counselling matters, and that talk therapy can influence you and your abuser, and improve your self-esteem. I believe that nobody really knows the depth of depravity and cunning that your abuser is applying to your spirit. This focus on your problems might lead you deeper into believing that the fault is yours. Be cautious when you search for help, and if you are being supported, trust your feeling that the problem should not be blamed on you. Certainly you may have personal issues to work on once you are free of his manipulation. You can then decide if you would benefit from some personal work, which will help you make use of your newfound freedom. Like some clients, you will probably discover that once you are left alone, and are free of his constant instruction and are able to listen to your intuitive voice, you will be able to live a satisfactory life, and cope with your difficulties and your successes without being compromised. Your honesty, loyalty, kindness and dedication do not need counselling, and your integrity and instinct are sufficient to allow you to enjoy your freedom. Should you have remaining difficulties, such as symptoms of trauma or depression, however, then I would certainly advise you to seek help.

11. Join a group of people who know about his mind-control

In groups, the participants may all be targets of mind-control. If they, or the group leaders, are not aware of this, participating in a group might be less useful for you. Abused women speak with the thoughts and language of their abusers. Their view of the world, and especially of their intimate relationships, has been contaminated by their abusers. If you listen to them discuss their experiences, what you will be listening to is a description of their overt abuse in the language of the abuser. What you will not hear is any detail of the hidden tactics of targeting, setting up and grooming, which are the foundation of the brainwashing that has already taken place. The controlled woman will probably confirm for you and others in the group that you are all being bullied in the same way. Many of these groups develop into sessions where women compete with each other to gain the sympathy of others. If you attend one of these groups, you may be encouraged to offer support to this process, and to offer sympathy to the group member whose story moves you most. Though all target women are affected in the same way, not all male intimate abusers use the same tactics, and not all abusers are equally lethal. The risk in a group of target women is that you will be measured by someone else's yardstick, or that you will be pressured to follow the route which others are on. Some of the group members may be free from abuse and may insist that they know how you can achieve it. Some of the group members may imply that your predicament is partly caused by your reluctance to take their advice. One of my clients attended such a group for more than seven years without any change happening for her.

Partners of psychephiles are mind-controlled

The reality of all women who live with psychephiles is the same. You are all denied the right to think for yourself. You are all equally controlled. The fact that some women experience more assaults and rapes is not due to the fact that some psychephiles are easier to live with. The level of open aggression and intimidation is directly related to the amount of resistance that the man encounters. If you do everything that he asks, if you tell him that he is right and that you are naive or stupid, if you convince him that he is a great lover, you will have a life that is relatively free of his anger. But if you decide not to cook his meals or not to organise his washing, if you decide not to share his bed or to accompany him when he wants you to, if you plead with him not to waste the resources of the family or to give some time to your children, he will develop, or intensify, a tactic which may get you to comply with his wishes and make you regret that you tried to defy him. He is not addicted to violence but he is only content when he is getting his own way. He reads the world around him instinctively and knows how to turn any situation to his advantage.

If you are in a group where other members are unaware of how they are manipulated, you may be criticised for behaving in ways that other women would not. One of my clients was condemned for making Christmas dinner for her abuser and the rest of her family. Another group member said that she had stopped making his dinner on Christmas or on any other day. It later emerged that this woman's Christmas day had been disrupted when the father would not allow the children to watch any television after dinner on that day. All her family had a miserable Christmas: her abuser had many tactics to use against her once she provoked him. My client, on the other hand, had a quiet day, and the level of tension in her house was no higher than usual. What most group members forget is that each woman is entitled to behave in any way that makes her life manageable. You are the only person who knows how to pacify your abuser. Being judged by other group members who think they know better is almost as hurtful as being condemned by your partner: you have a right to expect to be supported in these groups.

Power issues in the group

You may also be in a group where the facilitators are compromised either by fear of the abusers or by their desire to control the abused women in another way. If the group leaders are unfamiliar with the hidden tactics of mind-control, they may become constrained by the realisation that they know very little of his initial behaviour. This lack of knowledge will probably cause them to believe that they would never tolerate the kind of abuse that you are living with. I have met some of these well-intentioned group leaders, who see themselves as better than women who in their opinion, succumb to manipulation. Some of the groups are led by facilitators and prominent members who can drive their own agenda. This agenda may have less to do with your own well-being than with the personalities of the leaders. It takes extraordinary skill and patience to help all group members to arrive at a safe place, both in the group and in the wider world. Many women who engage with these groups become dependent on them and simply move from being controlled by their intimate partners to be being controlled by members of the group.

Some groups see through the abuser

There are some groups throughout the country that concentrate on the behaviour of you and women like you. Other groups are excellent in that they concentrate on the problem of his behaviour. These groups will help you unravel his tactics and show you that he behaves in a deliberate manner. These groups may also show you his motivation and his intention, which is to dominate you sexually. Some group members may challenge the idea that they are being dominated sexually, but every woman I have met who has been targeted, set up and groomed has lost her sexual integrity and is not allowed to negotiate the time or intensity of sexual activity. It can be very difficult for some women to admit this, and it can be very difficult for facilitators and other group members to discuss this issue in a group setting. Unless you find a group that appreciates that the problem is the sole responsibility of your partner, and that targets his attitude and behaviour, you may end up becoming more confused and despondent.

Some groups are seduced into helping him

One of the most powerful tactics the psychephile uses is to draw you into some process which he says will lead to his rehabilitation. Groups of academics and therapists can be groomed by the psychephile into drawing you into his game. He will convince these groups that his motives are good and that he regrets what has happened. These groups are fooled by his charm or his displayed innocence into feeling sorry for him, and they may put pressure on you to discuss things in a way that is not in your interest. One of these groups told me recently that they have never worked with psychopathic liars and that they do not get these kind of men in their groups. Another academic told me that the men needed the group as a therapy tool and that, when the group was in recess, the men were more likely to relapse. The idea that a psychephile could blame the absence of a regular group as a reason for assaulting his intimate partner is insulting to all men. The idea that the people running the group could be impressed by the man's honesty shows a dangerous level of naivety on their part. A local group publicly declared that the psychephiles needed their regular input and missed them when the groups were in recess. This naivety is widespread, and demonstrates how manipulative these men can be. It is also naive to believe that these men need therapy in order to help them to be respectful. The knowledge that a group of abused women are talking about him without diagnosing his behaviour is like manna to him, and simply feeds his entitlement and arrogance.

Summary

Confirmation

- Examine his behaviour for intention and effect
- He knows how much abuse to apply to you
- He knows the effect of any abusive behaviour on you

Accept that his behaviour is deliberate

- He can change his position to protect himself
- His emotional expressions are contrived

Observe the re-grooming

- He uses tactics that have worked in the past
- He instinctively uses new tactics if they are needed

Admit that his behaviour is beyond belief

- You will not be able to explain exactly what happens to you
- Your friends will not know that your mind is being controlled

Go to a counsellor who will protect your mind

- Find a counsellor who knows what will help you
- Get an accurate diagnosis of your abuser

Join a group of people whose minds are free

- Find a group who are not controlled by the voices of intimate abusers or by domineering members

Chapter Eight

Steps 12-15: Autonomy

12. Listen to your own instinctive voice
Right and wrong

Before you met your abuser, you were probably able to distinguish between right and wrong. You would know intuitively if some behaviour was good or bad, healthy or dangerous. Like most young adults, you may have had some doubts about your ability in this area, but in hindsight you will probably agree that you were right more often than you were wrong. You may also recall that you had the ability to recover when you were wrong. Like most young people, you began to learn from your mistakes and tried to improve your actions and your reasoning.

You also had an instinctive ability to assess the behaviour of others. Children seem to develop this ability at about age ten, defined by my religion as 'the age of reason'. Young people can become judgemental and uncompromising about the behaviour of others. They tend to view actions as either black or white, and have not developed an adult sense of what we grownups call grey areas. I invite you to listen to your childlike voice, which will tell you clearly when his behaviour is wrong. Try to avoid being seduced by his invitation to consider his grey areas of explanations and excuses. Your adult friends may also invite you into these areas of excuses. As I write this, I am reminded of a family-therapy session I had with a father, a mother and four of their children. The father had been abusive, violent and had repeatedly raped his wife. His eldest son,

106

who did not attend the session, had vowed to kill his father if he continued to abuse the mother. The youngest child, aged nine, had witnessed his mother being dragged out of his bed at knifepoint and pulled by her hair back to the master bedroom. The father dominated the initial part of the session, and when I invited the mother and the older children to speak they were reticent and uncertain. When the ten-year-old spoke, he was clear and precise. 'Please daddy,' he said, 'stop hurting mammy.' The child had made a clear assessment and a realistic demand.

You wanted to be right

I believe that your ability to review your own life and your interest in self-improvement were part of the reason that you were targeted by your abuser. If you were careless, or if you were satisfied with how you were, he would have found it difficult to motivate you into minding him as he wished. He might have tried to get you to spend your energy on him, and he would have abandoned you if he realised that you were not motivated or uninterested in meeting his needs. The fact that the psychephile stayed with you is a clear indication of your talents and commitment. You had all the ability to lead a healthy life and you also had the ability to follow your gut instinct, which was sufficient for you to cope with the world around you. This instinctive clarity was clouded by your abuser, and caused you to excuse his bad behaviour and blame yourself for his abuse. Even your arguments of what he does are considered in this manner.

He questioned your instinctive thinking in ways that made you challenge your own principles. He eroded the quick and accurate judgements that you were able to make readily before you met him, and replaced your intuition with confusion and doubt. Instead of allowing you to use your powers of discernment, he skilfully drew you into discussions and arguments where, instead of making quick and accurate decisions, you were forced into long-winded and circular debates that got you nowhere. Instead of being assured and energetic, you spent your time trying to make sense of his forceful opinions and twisted logic. These debates are based on, and driven by, fear. The underlying message is that you should get it right, and that, if you get it wrong, bad things will happen to you. Occasionally you will get the sense that something better will happen, if you can make sense of his logic and behave correctly. But this is not the end-goal of these arguments. The primary end-goal of the twisted debates and logic-bending is to push you into a corner, where all odds are against any other action; this will serve to keep you confused, afraid and controlled.

Because being in general control in your life and feeling well respected is desired by all of us, and certainly is part of what we should be able to expect, other people will automatically assume that your partner is also entitled to be in control of his life, and to be respected, in spite of his perceived failings. The abusive man will not see the extreme extent to which he demands and pursues these rights, because when other people are around, he is able to tone down his extreme stance and appear more normal and balanced. Since others judge him as they would anyone else, they assume that he takes your needs and wants into consideration, as they and the vast majority of people would. Only you know the force of his domination, and only you realise that you will never be equal to him in his eyes. He cannot allow you to influence him because he is terrified that you will gain access to his inner world. He is reluctant to enter that world himself because he knows how dark it is, but he prefers the darkness rather than allowing you to shine a light on it.

He tells you that you are wrong

Both your intuitive and your analytical thought-processes have been invaded and disrupted by the psychephile in your life. He has colonised your slow and analytical thinking to such an extent that he is able to dominate the processes you use to arrive at your decisions. He is present in your dreams and night-mares, he dominates your hopes and your plans, he draws you into conversations with him even when he is not physically present, because you never stop considering how he would react to you, and he never reassures you or supports your opinions. By keeping you mentally busy in your own slow-thinking process, he has managed to separate you from your own intuition. He has become so forceful in your mind that he has flooded your thoughts with his instructions and has denied you the opportunity to measure your intuition against his ideas. If you have been under his influence for a long time, you may have abandoned the hope of ever thinking clearly again, and replaced that hope with the fear of losing your mind. You will begin to believe that you are never right, and that your own thoughts are confused. Initially you will keep these thoughts to yourself, and gradually you will have fewer and fewer of your own ideas.

He dominates your thinking

Your own instinctive voice may be completely hidden, and you may spend most of your time trying to analyse what is happening. While he dominates your thoughts, you will be unable to make sense of yourself. You will wallow in doubt, confusion, anxiety and self-criticism, all of which he has implanted and cultivated. When you try to talk to yourself in the privacy of your heart, his voice will disrupt your conversation. When you are overcome with fear or terror, his voice will orchestrate your distress. You may already be unsure of your mental capacity, and may have abandoned your memory and accepted his recall. You may have already acknowledged that the mental torture he inflicts on you is as damaging and soul-destroying as any rape or physical assault.

Begin to listen to and to follow your intuition

If you can find a small but free corner of your mind, you may be able to regain your own intuitive thinking, and tell yourself that nobody deserves to suffer like you. You may recall a time, in years gone by, when you would advise your friends and siblings not to tolerate the abuse that you are living with. You may look at your own daughter and pray that she will not be seduced into living with a psychephile. These instinctive thoughts can open up a pathway for you and develop a lifeline to your own intuition. By encouraging yourself to have these internal conversations with your own intuition, you may begin to feel that the tension in your stomach is diminishing as the voice of your gut is being heard. I suggest that, when you are alone, you allow yourself to recognise this feeling and to appreciate the brief peace that it brings to you. If you begin to acknowledge the benefits of this exercise, you may continue to develop it until it becomes natural to you.

Painful lesson

When you access your instinct again, you will begin to recognise that you have been living with a liar and a conman. This can be a very traumatic exercise, and you may not wish to acknowledge his goal of controlling and hurting you. It is difficult to admit that the man you live with wants to destroy you. As you re-examine your relationship, you may realise that your life is even more pain-ful than you want to admit. You may recall events and emotions that you had hidden from yourself. These experiences needed to be hidden so that you could continue to survive. Your psyche might now want you to deal with these mem-ories, and your recall may be haunted by troublesome flashbacks. This review of your relationship needs to be slow and cautious, as getting complete recall in a short time may be overwhelming. The review may also be painful, but it has the value of diagnosing the source and level of your unease. This diagnosis is necessary if you are to develop a successful therapy and a lifelong cure.

Your instinct will eventually guide you into ignoring his lies and reconnect-ing with your initial thoughts. You can begin this process in secret: your abuser need not, **indeed must not,** know that you are reconnecting with your own instinct and beginning to see his behaviours in a clearer way. Your instinct is your best asset when it comes to your own safety. Talk to it and listen to it, and when it is safe, begin to follow its guidance.

13. Accept your instinct without examining it

Small steps without too much thought

When you begin to listen to your instincts, it is useful to act rather than to think about your initial decision. Beginning with small steps, you can test your instinctive thinking by setting yourself tasks that are private to you and that only you can evaluate. You might travel a different route to work or to visit family members when you are alone. The feeling of stepping outside your routine can be exciting as well as frightening, but the value of doing so is in the realisation that what you are doing is normal. You will become aware of the extent of his control when you take a little diversion from his instructions. You may prefer to do the family shopping on a particular day; moving this chore to a different day occasionally may give you a sense of freedom. You may go to bed at different times or cook meals that you have never tried before. There are many other ways that you can make small changes to your routine. You will begin to feel excited by your decisions and to realise that his control is destroying you. You will also start to grow more confident in your ability to make decisions. This confidence is a delicate flower and needs to be cultivated and propagated, but it also needs to be hardy enough to prosper in the dark. You may take a moment longer to reply to an e-mail or a text message from a friend. Try out different wordings in your head before you reply. The practice helps you see the difference between rigid, stuck, automatic actions, and decisions you make when you feel more flexible and free. Even a tiny trial which gives you a sense of unexpected freedom, will help you in the tougher moments, when you feel limited in your thinking due to fear or confusion, and will help you better recognise the difference between rigid and flexible responding better.

Do not try to explain to anyone

It is advisable that these little experiments remain very private. Even your children or your best friends do not need to know that you are behaving differently. Because your supportive people have little idea of the mind-control that he has over you, they will be unconvinced that you need to unravel his influence in a secret way. They will want to enter into debates and discussions with you which will allow them to take over the role of your abuser and be critical of your intuition. They may dismiss the need for small steps and encourage you to make a big leap. They may criticise your hesitancy and fail to acknowledge your achievements. The only person who may be of help to you is someone who recognises your integrity and supports you in making your own intuitive decisions. These people are very rare, and it may be best to keep your thoughts and small satisfactions private. Developing your own inner world will encourage your instinct to begin to express itself and will allow you to trust it, as you did before you came under the spell of your abuser.

Because the psychephile who controls your behaviour is skilled at drawing conclusions from very little information, he may appear to know that there are some small changes occurring in the family routine. Though it will be difficult for you, it might be helpful if you try to agree with him. Rather than justify your little freedoms, you might consider admitting that you are becoming confused and forgetful. This development will be like music to his ears, as it was always his intention to disrupt your ability to think and remember.

Learn from mistakes

You may be convinced that you are stupid and have lost the ability to learn from your mistakes. By going with your own fast thinking, you will begin to realise that your intuition is usually right and that, on the rare occasions that your first thoughts were wrong, you can still manage the outcome of any action you might take. It is possible that you will begin to learn that you can cope with your own intuition even when the outcome of your decision is different from what you expected. Because of your strength and your basic integrity, you can deal with negative outcomes and learn from your experiences. This ability has been silenced by the psychephile and you have spent a long time believing that you are inadequate or even useless. When you were a young woman, before you met your psychephile, you knew that you could make instant decisions that were usually right. You may even recall a time when your gut told you to be careful of this man. You might be angry with yourself for staying with him or going back to him after splitting up with him.

Our ability to learn depends on how well we store information in the moment something is there to be learned, and how well we retrieve this stored information later. The very nature of the interactions with the abuser is the opposite: impressionistic, heightened, narrow-focused. What led you there, and what can bring you out of it, is blurred to you. This is true for both the positive moments and the negative ones. When you feel completely engulfed in passion, your judgement of how solid and lasting this emotion is, will be blurred. When you are extremely afraid, your judgement of how solid and lasting the moment will be, is equally blurred. You are not able to store enough useful information, and you are unable to retrieve any useful learning.

What I hope you will begin to notice is that most of what you do is good, but it is seldom enough. His demands are never met, because he does not want you to meet them. Even if you did something better than he requested, he can raise the bar and tell you that you have failed. The only mistake that you may make is to believe that he will eventually be satisfied. When you review the pattern of the relationship, you will see that he is not interested in your success or appreciative of your efforts. When you learn that you can never do enough, you may begin to re-think the motivations that drive you. You may learn to begin to do things for yourself.

Your abuse is because of him, not you

The fact that you stayed in the relationship is not a measure of your decision-making powers but a clear indicator of the extraordinary skill and persistence of every psychephile. You might not want to admit it, but your partner is exceptionally cunning, and always alert for ways to improve his life. His cunning is part of his instinctive behaviour, and he is arrogant enough to believe that he will get what he wants, because he knows how to colonise your thinking. He becomes more arrogant with each little success, until he can move effortlessly from one tactic to another. By accumulating a string of tactics that overcome your resistance, he can pick and choose whichever one is most effective at any time. He can instinctively switch away from any tactic that is not working, until he finds one that is successful. This store of effective and immediately available tactics is vital to him, and is so extensive that he appears to be a step ahead of everyone else. Trying to anticipate his next move is seldom effective, because he can manoeuvre the conversation in unexpected ways, and even change the topic in an instant. It can be helpful if you observe this talent when your abuser is in conversation with others. You will notice how easily and quickly he changes the focus of the conversation, and how effortlessly he can shift the listener onto an issue that is of his choosing. He does this especially if he is talking to people who might criticise or judge him.

He may get worse

As the connection you are making with your own instinct is delicate, and the trust you have in it needs to be renewed, it is better if your initial moves take place in your inner world, and that you do not subject your instinctive reactions to initial scrutiny. This may also apply to your own way of thinking; you allow yourself to make snap decisions, even if the snap decision is to do nothing. It took months, maybe even years, for your abuser to separate you from your intuitive self; reconnecting with it is best done without his knowledge, as he can disrupt the process. He can also destroy any progress you may have made, and even develop tighter controls if he is alerted to any change in your way of thinking. I do not want you to start out on the steps to freedom and then find that you have been pulled back into a darker and stronger prison.

Do not ignore your fear

Your abuser has invaded your thoughts; when you move these thoughts to your analytic mind, you will commence a monologue with him in your head. This is a discussion that you cannot win, as he is never reasonable or agreeable. Taking his opinions on board will result in you becoming confused and anxious; therefore, it is much more healthy for you to make your own decisions. Your ability to act on your own decision may be constrained by your fear, and you may wish to confine your initial decisions to yourself and only act on them if it is safe to do so. This fear is healthy and real, and it should be used to modify your actions. As you begin to reconnect with your instinct, you will begin to recognise that his behaviour is a game filled with arrogance and lies. This awareness may help you realise that any effort you make to influence him is wasted. Your fear may also alert you to the realisation that he can be more dangerous when he is challenged or threatened. Your fear can stop you from telling him he is wrong, threatening to report him to the authorities, or suggesting that you might leave him. This instinctive fear is invaluable and can be developed to keep you free of abuse.

Your instinct knows best

This awareness will also allow you to conclude that he has no interest in your well-being. This will encourage you to follow your instincts and be cautious around him, and avoid fuelling his sense of being let down. When I started to work with this issue, I was baffled when one of my colleagues told me that she had agreed with a client that the safest thing for her to do was to return to the marriage bed, which she had left some months previously. As a man, I found this move abhorrent: I could not accept that any woman should be obliged to renew the degradation which had caused her to leave his bed in the first place. But my colleague taught me that the woman needed to do whatever she could to make her world safe, and to recognise that this woman was an expert in staying sane and alive.

When you hear your gut telling you to act in a particular way, it is best to follow it, even though it may not make sense to you. Your intuition is a very old part of your being: you developed your ability to act instinctively before you knew how to analyse issues. It is instinct that allows animals to survive in the wild and encourages the flock of starlings to remain nervous while they **forage for food** on your lawn. These creatures have a well-developed instinct for survival; they do not analyse information but act first, even when it emerges that there may have been little initial danger.

Acting instinctively when you do your chores, when you are interacting with your children, when you meet your family or friends, or when you go to your job may be good for you. Acting instinctively with your abuser will always be the safest thing for you to do, even though it may have short-term negative effects on your psyche. You do not need to think before you act, as your thinking will be influenced by him, and you will probably end up doing what he would like you to do. There will be moments when you have time to think twice, however. I believe that you get this extra space to think because your mind senses that there are options. Grab these moments when you can. Use them to practise listening to your own voice.

14. You do not need to justify your decisions
All kind women believe that they will be accepted

Very few people know what it is like to be brainwashed by an intimate partner. This lack of understanding is what makes it difficult for friends to accept some of your decisions. It becomes impossible to justify your plans, and they may pick holes in your explanations. As I mentioned in the last chapter, one of my clients needed to return to the marital bed until she could arrange to leave home. Because I had learned that she was right to do this, I supported her. Her friends and family were completely against her decision. She is safe today.

You may have wasted years of energy trying to explain yourself to your abuser. It is unlikely that you ever felt that he accepted your explanation. You probably found that he didn't seem to be listening to what you were saying, and that he would make a different point to the one you wanted to make. You can no doubt remember many times when you were clear and precise and yet were made to feel that you did not explain yourself properly. This tactic of attacking your explanation is used by both abusive fathers and rebellious teenagers. If you attempt to justify your decision by going into an explanation of your thinking, you will find yourself undermined, and your clarity and your reasonableness ignored.

This undermining is achieved by presenting a different logic or by expanding your guilt. Your teenage children will try to make you realise that you don't understand their world, and that your thinking is out of touch with the reality of their lives. They will also attempt to play on your uncertainty and challenge your unreasonableness. They will focus on the guilt that you carry as a result of being unable to protect them from the manipulation of their father or the guilt generated by your belief that you are the cause of the tension in your home, and help expand this guilt by criticising your parenting skills. If you make a clear and simple statement of your decision to your children, and resist being drawn into a protracted debate, you will protect your decision and avoid being swayed into changing your mind. Your children will also grow to acknowledge your honesty and confidence.

Similarly, your intimate partner relishes your attempts to explain your decisions. The more you try to explain, and the more you try to have him concur, the more you will end up in a quagmire of confusion and guilt. Your confusion will be orchestrated by his instinctive ability to challenge your explanation, and to highlight other options. Your guilt will be fed by your inability to get through to him, and by the outcome, which is either a compromise or a complete abandonment of your initial position.

He does not want to understand you but to undermine you

The psychephile wants to draw you into a conversation on your reasons for making a particular decision. He is more skilled than your children in encouraging you to give a detailed explanation of how you arrived at your decision. He may claim that he is uncertain about the outcome, or anxious about any unforeseen effects, and seduce you into revealing your thought-process. Or he may revert to name-calling in a way that causes you to impress upon him your ability to make a simple decision. He may be confident enough to reject your plan without any discussion, knowing that you will pursue him in an attempt to get him to cooperate with you. He has many effective processes by which he gets you to detail the reasoning behind your decision. Once he becomes aware of your analysis, and the intuition which you have used in relation to any issue, he will begin to undermine your thought-process. He will challenge the effectiveness of your instinct by reminding you of any unsuccessful decisions that you made in the past. He will remind you that unless you give every action a reasonable amount of consideration, you might make another mistake and, in doing so, may disrupt the peace of the family. He will explain that any hasty action is risky, and that you need to give consideration to even the simplest of decisions. This tactic of constantly dismissing your intuition will gradually erode any confidence you had in your ability to think instinctively, and will cause you to ignore your immediate response to any situation.

Once he has achieved the ability to groom you into overlooking your intuition, he will invite you to elaborate on your analytical thinking and to engage in a debate with him. He may challenge any statement that you make, or he may present a completely different view of the issue. He will generate confusion and may even dismiss your intelligence. He will invade your mind and flood you with his logic and his language. He will be persistent and unyielding and will wear you down until you concede to his wishes. By keeping you on this constant treadmill, he will dismantle your rational thought-process and gain confidence in his ability to regulate any decision you plan to make. He will use your own conversation to control you by picking holes in your explanations.

You are entitled to make some decisions

If you wish to reverse the brainwashing that you have endured, you might begin by keeping some of your thoughts hidden. You can begin to make simple decisions that he may not observe. By reconnecting with your intuition, you will regain a little confidence in your instinctive wisdom, and the basic skill you have to recognise right from wrong. When you were a younger woman, you had the ability to make quick and effective decisions. Your intuition was accurate, even though you may have ignored it sometimes. When you met your abuser, you may have got some warning signals from your instinct, but because you couldn't justify acting on them, you went deeper into an abusive relationship. You may have tried and failed to have your concerns discussed, you may even have discussed them and been assured that your concerns were unfounded, or you may have been told that your anxieties were a product of your own insecurities. But you were seldom comforted by a real commitment that he would address the basis of your concerns. Like some of my clients, you may have been seduced by a psychephile who was so skilful that your instinct didn't issue any warning, and you rushed into an intimate relationship without considering any potential risks.

You would have learned from early in the relationship that you would seldom win an argument, and that your intelligence and ideas were not as good as his. This lesson was repeated every time you tried to be heard, and you began to believe in his twisted logic. His logic was twisted by his desire to invade your mind and by the manipulation and lies that he repeatedly used.

You can stop giving him access to your mind

Your explanations were the pathway that he used to gain access to your mind. As you increased your efforts to justify yourself, he gained invaluable information as to how your inner world functioned. He developed that information each time he drew you into a debate about your reasoning or your decisions. While you were being abused, you lost contact with your own instinctive voice. It is time to quietly reconnect with your own intuition – and, at least initially, without anyone being aware that you are doing so. You can practise making small decisions and acting on them. You can begin to say 'yes' or 'no' without trying to justify your reasoning. You can begin to develop the habit of repeating your decision when asked for an explanation. You can experiment with doing this with people who do not question you or with people who are not important in your life.

You can take a stand with your siblings or your children and repeat your position as often as is necessary. You may notice that there is a whole group of people who wish to influence your behaviour. Your friends, parents, siblings and work colleagues may all be surprised when you keep to your initial decision. You may be labelled as stubborn or odd by those who want you to act in the old familiar way. Very few people want you to change, because then they will lose their ability to manipulate you. Because you are the target of a psychephile, I believe that you are fundamentally kind and that many people have already taken advantage of your kindness. So I would recommend that you begin to develop your ability to protect yourself by only being kind to those who appreciate you. I make this recommendation to all my clients who are kind and are taken advantage of by others who are not so kind. Like many of my clients, you may be able to decide quickly who to keep on your list, and to strike off the self-centred people who take you for granted.

Be cautious about revealing your small changes

If you start slowly to protect your own instinct, you will grow in confidence and will trust your intuition to help you make prompt and useful decisions. During this process, I would suggest that you continue to keep responding to your abuser in ways that minimise your risks. Your recovery may be slow and your confidence may be brittle, so that he can undermine any progress you make. He may also intensify his monitoring and may subject you to more intense scrutiny. The result could be that your life becomes more compromised, your options decrease and the bars of your prison become stronger.

If you go through the cycle of hope and despair on a number of occasions, you are likely to become de-energised and helpless. By contrast, as you clear your mind and begin to hear again your own thought-process, you will realise that you have all the ability required to make decisions that are useful for you. You will also begin to notice that you can cope with difficulties and modify your plans as time goes by. There is very little value in escaping from your abuser, only to hand over your life to other controllers. Many of my clients have escaped the clutches of an abuser only to end up trapped in another abusive relationship, and often one that is worse than the previous one. Some of my clients have repeated this depressing cycle more than once. I would not wish this for you, and I would suggest that one small step you should take to resist further abuse is to decline to explain your decisions. You have earned the right to live the life that suits you best, and your instinct contains most of the wisdom you need. Make small changes in your thinking, and practise small behavioural changes which remain hidden.

15. Talk about other things, not him

Talking about him keeps him alive in your mind

Talking about your abuser – what he says and does – will not lessen the abuse that he practises on you. He will continue to control you and may become more alert if he realises that you have broken the secret of his behaviour. This escalation may encourage you to try and find help in managing his dominance. You may talk to others in some detail about him.

You may also confide in your friends and your family in the hope that they will understand the depth of your distress. His behaviour will dominate your conversation because you do not know what else to talk about. You have lost interest in the topics that you used to discuss. You find it hard to hear about the successes of your friends. You will probably have begun to withdraw from some of your circle of friends, and you may also be hesitant to socialise with colleagues. Your friends may have told you that you have changed, and this change is probably noticeable in what you talk about. Your conversations become limited and they also become unhelpful. Each time you introduce him into your conversation, you allow him to influence your thoughts. He may even have the effect of raising your level of tension or of giving you stomach sensations. It is inevitable that, as you experience these physiological reactions, you inscribe your reactions into the fibre of your body. The more you are aware of these sensations, the more difficult it will be to free yourself from him.

You bring his voice with you

By talking about him, and your inability to improve him, you fill your thoughts with self-doubt. You remind yourself repeatedly that you are unable to manage his moods and his abuse, or you think incessantly about what you can do to end it. You may even convince yourself that you must try harder, and you waste your mental energy on devising new strategies which inevitably do not succeed. He dominates your thinking and invades your conversation. You begin to lose faith in your opinions, and you question your judgement and memory. You will have begun to express his thoughts and find yourself defending his opinions. You may begin to share his worldview and to modify the principles by which you lived before you met him. The language that you use will be different, and the attitudes that you express will not be the same as those you expressed when you were young. You will bring him into your conversation repeatedly, in order to justify your statements and to explain your changed opinions. His success is complete if he can manipulate your conversation even when he is not present.

His presence in your mind could be described as a mental virus. He should not be there, because he wants to damage your thinking. If you need to talk about him, you will agitate this virus and set it spinning through your thoughts. You will be reminded of his abuse and will be re-connected with your anxiety. You will experience the familiar feelings of frustration, confusion and fear. You may find yourself engaging in conversations with him in your head and developing new ways of talking to him. It is possible that you spend most of your waking hours thinking about him, so it becomes inevitable that he takes over your conversations.

He will be pleased to know that you are talking about him

Being in an abusive relationship means that the man who targeted you is the one with the problem; talking about him will not help him. While the man has access to your thinking, any talking about him may make you more afraid or more angry but will have no impact on him. Repeating stories of his abusive behaviour will expand them in your mind, and eventually these stories will overwhelm your thinking and allow his voice to control you, even when he is not present. Most therapists, friends or family members have no idea that you have been brainwashed, and think they are listening to your rational thoughts when in reality you are expressing his opinions. When you are talking about him, you fill your mind with his thoughts; you may hear his voice in your head and experience fear in your gut. He is reassured if he knows that you are using his language and his descriptions to describe the difficulties you have in the relationship. Your recovery will begin when you are able not to have these conversations, even for a short period of time.

If you change the topic you will enjoy being with friends

If you and your supporters stop talking about him, you will begin to express your own ideas, and this conversation will allow you to begin to speak with your own instinctive voice. You may start to recognise that there are other important issues for you to talk about. You may find yourself taking a more active part in other people's conversations. One of my clients said that she found herself laughing for the first time in years when she met some of her friends and they all agreed to not mention her partner during the evening. She also noticed how her friends were more relaxed in her company.

As you keep him away from your conversation, you will realise that he does not deserve to be part of your life with your friends and family. You will notice a benefit for you in that you will be able to distract yourself from him. The ability to form opinions and make decisions will re-emerge, and you will get small glimpses of the freedom that you deserve. My clients also report that they find that the exercise of keeping him out of their conversation indicates to them the extent of his dominance, and reassures them that they can regain control of their own thinking.

The real value of this exercise is that you can do it without his knowledge and appreciate the benefits to you without telling him. Practising ways to reconnect with your thoughts and opinions will indicate to you that, even though you have been out of touch with your intuition, it is not damaged but merely hidden. As you allow these thoughts and opinions to influence your thinking, and as you begin to express them in your conversation, you will be relieved to learn that you are the same capable person that you were before you met him. Not talking about him will have no influence on his behaviour, but it will reduce his influence on you.

Summary

Autonomy

Listen to your own instinctive voice

- Your instinct remains intact but has been ignored.
- When you follow your instinct, you are being the real you.

Try not to analyse this voice

- When you try to analyse your instinct, it will be silenced by his voice, which is in your analytical mind.
- It is good to regain confidence in making your own quick decisions and beginning to act on them.

Hide the reasons behind your decisions

- Trying to build an explanation for your decisions will lead you into analysing them.
- Explaining them will give him an opportunity to question them and to raise doubts in your mind.

Talk about other things

- If you need to talk about him. he will be alive in your mind, and his influence may grow.
- Your family and friends will prefer it when you talk about other issues.

Chapter Nine

Steps 16 to 20: Self-priority

16. Put yourself first
Self-care is essential – so that you can care for others

Most parents would like their children to grow up to be caring and generous adults. We are bombarded with quasi-religious messages which encourage us to sacrifice our own well-being and focus on the well-being of others. Women are further encouraged by religion and culture to actively put their intimate partner first. All these messages distort the truth, which is that we are tasked with caring for others in the way that we care for ourselves. If you have spent your adult life looking after others – parents, siblings, children and spouses – it is unlikely that you know how to care for yourself. You may have spent your energy on the treadmill of life, which he controls, and recognise that your resources are being depleted. As you become drained (described by my clients as 'at the end of my tether'), you may feel more and more inadequate, while your abuser increases his demands. His ability to invade your thoughts and colonise your energy is based on your kindness and loyalty. If you were innately selfish or demanding, he would have left you for an easier target.

From your initial encounters with him, he has exploited your good nature and forced you into giving him priority in your life. He has used your attractive personality traits against you and managed to become the priority in your life. He has been helped by your upbringing and has built on your belief that caring for yourself is somehow wrong. He has focused on your sense of guilt and your abhorrence of appearing selfish. He has put himself at the centre of your world and reduced you to a bit-player in the drama of his life. He may have encouraged you to see yourself as insignificant and forced you to believe that you are not worthy of care. He will probably convince you that your children are more important than you; he may even persuade you that the family pets deserve more care than you.

If he has a career or a social life, he will oblige you to see yourself as less important than these activities. He will use you as an attachment to his public persona and make you feel like a prop, to bolster his social status. He may glorify you or demean you in public; you know that he is doing so for his own benefit. He may eventually make you feel worthless and prove to you that you do not deserve recognition as a person. He will steal your sense of femininity and force you to see yourself as an object rather than a person. You will begin to accept his assessment of you and convince yourself that you deserve your mistreatment. You will lose your self-confidence and self-respect and will eventually accept that you are not worthy of self-care.

One of my clients had suffered severe physical and sexual abuse for eighteen years and did not even consider that she had a right to leave her marriage. She was found in her back garden naked and whimpering by a neighbour, who had been detected a smell of smoke. He saw her husband burn all her clothes, including nightclothes, which he had torn from her body. He also found her two children standing at the back door in a trance-like state. The neighbour delivered some clothes to the woman the following morning and introduced her to me some days later. She tried to convince me that her husband's rage was justified because she felt she spent too much money on clothes. When I explored this with my client, I learned that she did not own a coat and that he had bought her every dress that she wore so that she could look well when they attended his business functions. The only clothes she had bought without him were underwear and some warm jumpers. She tried to convince me that her husband was a good provider and that she should be grateful for the clothes she had. My revelations did not help her see that she was being abused, but when she heard from her neighbour about the distressed state of her children, she left her marriage and the family home and began a new life without any contact with him. She is married to a very different man today and has a successful business.

Putting 'me' first

My clients readily admit that they do not know how to care for themselves. They confess that they never thought they were entitled to make themselves a priority in their own lives. I use the analogy of the cabin-crew member who tells parents that if the plane gets into difficulties, the adults should put on their oxygen masks before tending to the children. Any woman who lives with a psy-chephile is operating in a crisis and is obliged to protect her own ability to think clearly: she needs to retain her mental faculties even in a crisis. The purpose of the instruction is to alert the parent to the value of caring for oneself so that the parent will be better able to fulfil her duties, and the children will benefit from her clarity and composure.

Because the nature of every mind-controlled woman is dominated by her kindness and concern for others, it is unhelpful to encourage her to care for herself if she believes that to do so would be selfish. It is easier for her to con-sider the concept if she can recognise the benefit that doing so will have for her family. If you have children, you want what is best for them. You probably believe that you are responsible for the level of tension in your home, and the fear and the chaos generated by your partner. You may begin to become anxious about how your children will grow up, and whether they will repeat the behaviours of their parents. These concerns will cause you to increase your efforts to manage your partner and to protect your children from being dam-aged by his behaviour. By putting on your own 'oxygen mask', you will think more clearly and act more decisively for the benefit of all your family.

You cannot compete with him

The psychephile in your life does not want this to happen, and will persistently anticipate your tactics and undermine any progress you make. Your efforts will run out of energy and you will find it increasingly difficult to generate new strategies because of your lack of success. You will eventually begin to believe that you do not have enough energy to keep going, and the burden of survival may become overwhelming. This sensation of being overwhelmed may lead you to contemplate running away or imagining the possibility of him leaving you. It has also caused some of my clients to bury themselves in unhealthy habits or to consider the ultimate escape of suicide. Sadly, some of my clients have died either by their own hand or been murdered by a psychephile. These deaths are a dramatic display of the ultimate control that the abuser feels is his entitlement.

The man who is abusive in the context of an intimate relationship is convinced that your life is only of value insofar as it ministers to his needs and enhances his image. He is unable to acknowledge that you have a right to a safe emotional existence because he regards you as less than human, and therefore as inferior to him. He is unwilling to admit that you have a good nature and a graciousness that is attractive. He may even be anxious about your ability to challenge him, and may be frightened that you will access his vulnerability. If you accept that you are a lesser person than him, he has won: he will constantly remind you of his superiority.

He may win

Unless you permit yourself to do only what is good for you, the tiredness you experience will eventually overwhelm you. As I have already suggested, it may be useful to review your daily routine and to continue to do most of the things you are doing, but to do these tasks not because you must but because you want to. Making a separate dinner for your husband can be a huge effort if you do so because he insists. It might make the task a little easier if you begin to make this meal because it is what you want to do. It will be less draining on your energy if you do so in the knowledge that he is trying to wear you down and is pleased to hear you complain. If you do not complain about his demands and carry out these tasks because you want to, he will become confused and anxious about his ability to distress you. Giving instructions and making demands are effortless to him and do not drain his energy, while trying to meet his ever-changing goals will leave you exhausted.

Do things for yourself

If you change the reason why you do something, you may be better able to appreciate the outcome. You will begin to measure the success of any event in terms of whether it was good for you or not. Your attitude of self-care can be developed silently, and your partner may be unaware of your new way of thinking. This practice of self-priority can become your hidden mantra, and can begin the process of reward which has been denied you. When you can lie in bed at night and say to yourself that you are glad you did something for yourself today, you may find that the outcome is personal and that the effort is less of a burden. You can also congratulate yourself for achieving the desired outcome of the small and simple tasks that you did willingly each day. The purpose of your routine becomes your own satisfaction, and you will begin to accept that your partner will never congratulate you. As you view each task differently, it will become evident that your partner is unlikely to express satisfaction and is more inclined to increase his demands.

17. Clarify your options
He has confused you

As you begin to regain your own intuition, you may realise that you have options and responsibilities. This realisation can come slowly, as the instinct that you developed as a child has been hidden for a long time. As you reconnect with it, you will recognise that you find it hard to trust it, and maybe even tend to dismiss it. Your lack of faith in your own judgement has been damaged by his incessant criticism. Even when you know you have been right and have predicted the outcome of any action, you have been bombarded with his view and have probably said that he was right. This denial of your own better judgement has led you to rely on his opinion and to lose the habit of making your own assessment. You may have got to the stage where you are convinced that judging issues is a waste of time and that you are so bad at making decisions that you no longer deserve the freedom to make up your own mind.

Follow your instinct

You and I can examine some options in the following chapter: you may have some of which I am unaware. Just because some helpful people may favour certain options over others does not mean that anyone knows best. As you reconnect with your intuition, you can practise making your own decisions. Once you change your focus back to your instinct, you will have arrived at the end of the tunnel. I have often recommended to my clients that, as they emerge from the tunnel of abuse, they take some time to adjust to the sunlight. When you begin to trust your instinct over small issues, you will be able to rely on your decision-making process. You will also be able to cope with the outcome of your own strategies. You can be hopeful, in the certainty that the future is manageable, even if it is not always easy, and your instinct is right most of the time, and that you can learn how to follow it.

Value your opinions

The sense that you do not have a right to your opinion, and your instinct is wrong, may have led you to a place where you see yourself as less than human. You may believe that you are incapable of being useful and that your opinions and decisions are worthless. You may have lost your belief in your status as a woman, partner and mother, and your sense of animal survival, and accept that you deserve to be abused. Your culture or religion may encourage you to believe that you are second-class and that you choose a life of suffering by having freely got into a relationship with a psychephile. It may take some time for you to begin to see yourself as fully human, to convince yourself that you do not deserve to suffer at the hands of the man you are willing to love, and to step back from the treadmill and begin to notice how he controls you. In short, it may take some time for you to begin to think that you are important.

Focus on yourself

If I can help, I would like to give you permission to focus on yourself. I would like to remind you of the golden rule, which is that you look after yourself the way you look after others. I would like to encourage you to look after yourself, not with the aim of making you self-centred, but with the goal of you regaining your mental health and becoming better able to care for the people in your life. Your children need and deserve at least one parent who is in tune with their emotional needs. They need that parent to have a clear picture of any manipulation that the psychephile might apply to them. They need one parent to keep them from being caught between warring parents, to help them resist any attempts the abuser might make to invade their minds and split their spirits, and to help guide them on the difficult path towards becoming an adult. They need one parent to convince them that manipulation and abuse have no place in an adult intimate relationship.

Can you help him?

You may find it difficult to accept, but the kindest act you can do for your abuser is never to let him abuse you again. By not letting him dictate your life, you will be giving him an opportunity to behave in a manly way. You will be giving him a chance to grow up and act like an adult, and not like a big child. All your attempts at influencing him up to now have failed because you have been ignored, and also because you have excused him and maybe even forgiven him. There is no valid excuse for your distress; by allowing him to repeat or intensify his bad behaviour, you are allowing him to become more arrogant and entitled. If he is not stopped, he will die believing that he was right and that the rest of the world was wrong. You will not be rewarded if you try to get him to grow up.

Give an example

If you have children, it would be good parenting to show them that no man or woman deserves to live a life of abuse and degradation. While you will have worked intensely at telling your children the difference between right and wrong, and have prayed that your children do not repeat the relationship of their parents, it will be much more effective if you show them that no woman, and no mother, deserves to be treated like a slave. Our children learn a lot from our example: if you act as though a wife deserves to be controlled, they may bring that attitude into their own intimate relationships.

Don't believe him

One of the powerful tactics used by your abuser to control you is to interpret and modify any information you may need. He will tell you what might happen if you talk to somebody or if you contact a statutory agency. He may tell you that your children will be taken into care or that, if you leave him, he will make sure that the children stay with him. He will try to persuade you that he will get the law to protect him, and that you will be left penniless and maybe homeless. He may also tell you that he might kill himself, or you or your children. All this information is designed to stop you from acting to protect yourself and your children. It is much more efficient to get your own information and to discuss your options with some professional people. Doing so does not mean that you are going to act, but it allows you to reduce your confusion. When you see things more clearly, you can begin to make decisions which best suit you.

18. Stay alert and afraid

He is never nice to you without a hidden agenda

Many of your advisors may suggest to you that you stop being afraid of your abuser, and some may even suggest that you stand up to him. It is dangerous even to think like that. Your abuser is a dangerous man who hides his deviousness behind a veneer of respectability. You will not be able to penetrate this veneer; in fact, all your efforts to placate him have already failed. While he has access to your inner life, he can manipulate you into letting your guard down. He may seem to support you by providing useful household goods, but will eventually withhold some of your money in order to pay for them. One of my clients took the delivery of a state-of-the-art electric cooker, only to find that the cost was put on the next utility bill. She had agreed that he could go to Spain for a week with his golfing friends before she realised that she would have to pay for the cooker.

Many of my friends and professional colleagues disagree with me on the question of whether he is sometimes well intentioned or is always following his own agenda. The test that you might apply is how it makes you feel when he appears to act in a loving way towards you. If your emotional response is tarnished by an uneasy feeling, it is unlikely that he is being nice to you. The people who know what he has done will not understand the effect his behaviour is having on you, and you may be obliged to hide your emotional anxiety because otherwise you may appear to be ungrateful. If he is a psychephile, your partner never notices if you are pleased or not, as his only concern is the benefit to himself. His self-absorption knows no bounds. Try to ask someone else, or a few people, how they feel when their partner behaves in a loving way towards them. Compare what they tell you to your own experience. Is it the same?

You may be told to stand up to him

It may be suggested to you that you withdraw some services in order for him to get the message that he cannot take you for granted. If you have tried to send any such signals already, you may have noticed that he has ignored some of them. He might pursue you for a time and try to bully you into submission, but if you hold your ground, he will intensify his demands on some other issue. If you decide not to cook his meals, for example, he will probably withdraw some or all of his contribution to the household budget. If you suggest that you no longer wish to be intimate with him, he may withdraw from the bedroom but continually put pressure on you to allow him back in. He may even try to be intimate with you, and demand that you give him his conjugal rights. I would always recommend that my clients do whatever it takes to remain alive and safe. Giving in to him might be very difficult, but in the short term it may the wisest thing to do. This means that you comply with his wishes, or that you appear to agree with his opinions. If you can do this while monitoring his intentions, you will begin to realise that he is always abusive and that what appears to be reasonable is just part of his grooming process.

Nobody else knows him like you

This process of assessing your best option is a very personal one. It requires that your intuition is sharp and that you are prepared to heed it. Because you have ignored your gut instinct for a long time, you will find that you are hesitant to trust it. As I have said already, you can deepen that trust by listening to it about little things initially. You can change some small patterns in your life and realise that your intuition is valid and that you have an opinion which is worth-while. You know how to mind your sanity, and you know how dangerous he can become when he is challenged. Small, unnoticed steps will allow you to develop your confidence and awareness. Your intuition needs to be constantly switched on and allowed to influence your immediate decisions at any time. When it is strong enough, it will drown out his voice in your head and encourage you to make the decisions that are best for you. You may do exactly as he would wish, or you may do something slightly or greatly different, but the key is that you act in a way that is most suitable for you. Acting quickly in your own interest will become more and more of a habit, and you will begin to identify your best option in any situation by staying alert. Only you can measure the risk involved in any change you make, as you are the only one with the knowledge of how he is when he closes the front door of your home. Also, you are the only person who will suffer if he becomes abusive.

If you feel you are in danger you are right

You live in circumstances that are risky, and you live with a psychephile who ignores the hurt he can cause you. For these reasons, being alert needs to include being alert to the danger you are in. You are probably convinced that his more gruesome threats are just talk, and that he would never kill you, or burn your house down, drown you in the river, harm your children or take his own life. You may be right, but some of my clients did not believe these threats either, and learned that they were wrong. Your confusion is caused by these threats being stated and then being dismissed by him when he tells you that he didn't mean them, or that you did not hear him properly and that he never threatened to do those things. Your instinct may be silent but you will notice the upheaval in your stomach when you think of what he said. This is your gut attempting to tell you that you are at risk and that he is capable of dangerous behaviour. Your head may not believe it, but your instinct is primed to assess any danger you may be in.

Fear of being exposed can make the abuser lethal

When the psychephile is cornered or about to be exposed, he can become irrational and lethal. When he begins to realise that his life's project is about to fail, he can lash out and do extraordinary damage. His sense of entitlement may lead him to believe that the person who is causing him so much grief deserves to be punished severely. His level of arrogance may convince him that he will suffer little or no consequence for his actions. Or he may believe that his life's work has been a failure, and that his attempt to subdue a woman has been a disaster. This 'catastrophic thinking' may lead him to lose interest in his own well-being. If a psychephile begins to think like that, he may behave in ways that are unpredictable. He may kill you and make it look as though you took your own life, he may take his own life and make you feel responsible, and in the most extreme cases he may kill you or your children before taking his own life. There may be times when you look into his eyes and realise that you do not know what is going on in his head.

Do not negotiate if you are about to act

If you are considering a breakup of the relationship, it is advisable that you do so secretly. You may recognise that you have been unable to negotiate your well-being with him over the years, and that any request you made to improve your life has been denied. This refusal will be far more entrenched if you attempt to negotiate a separation. If he has been unreasonable during your relationship, he may be more unreasonable during the breakup. It is a depressing reality that target women are at their most vulnerable when they begin to withdraw from their abuser. I would strongly suggest that you do not act without being protected from his reaction. I believe that this protection is the responsibility of the community around you, but my experience is that the community may fail you. I would again encourage you to clarify your options, listen to your intuition and only act when it is safe for you to do so.

One of my current clients came to me recently to tell me that she was moving out of the family home on the following Monday. Having endured several years of intimidation and abuse, she had finally decided to act. She had inherited another house, and had arranged to have all her property moved to this new home over the weekend. She had told her husband of her plans, in the hope that he would allow her to use his van at the weekend, as he did not need it. He agreed, and she arranged with her brothers to help her with the move. On the Saturday, he informed her that she could not use the van, as none of her brothers were insured to drive it, and that he would have them arrested if any of them tried to drive it. As he is a policeman, she realised that he had planned such a move. When she managed to get another van, he told her brothers that they could not enter her home, as it was his property and that he would arrest them for trespassing. Three weeks later, she had still not been able to access her property, even though she is in the new house and her children are being cared for by her sister.

There is an old Irish saying which loosely translates as 'May you be in heaven for two weeks before the devil finds out that you are dead'. I encourage my clients to act secretly, without giving their partner advance notice of their plans.

Another woman

The exception may be a man who already has access to another woman. While this man may dramatise his leaving, he may not destroy his existing family. This reprieve given to his family is not an indication of change or sorrow on his part for all the harm he has done, but a tactic to win favour and sympathy from his new target-woman. He can label you as a bitch and win sympathy from his new partner for all the abuse you gave him. He can use access to his children to convince his new partner of his good intentions and his heartache at being separated from them. He can gain more sympathy by demonstrating that the access arrangements are an example of your intentions to keep the children away from him. If you take a firm stand against this, he will consolidate his relationship with his new partner by discussing and developing a range of strategies to undermine your role. He may encourage his new partner to act as the child's parent and to undermine your authority.

He can get at you from a distance

Just because you do not share his bed, or he no longer lives in your house, does not mean that you are free or safe. He can access your home unless you have a barring order, and even then he can do a lot of harm before the police arrive. He can stalk you at your place of work or accost you when you are with your children. He can use court arrangements for access and maintenance to infiltrate your daily life from a distance. He can pester you with phone calls or texts to constantly change existing arrangements. He will do all of these things if he believes that he can get a reaction from you. If he can get you to show anger or resentment, he can use your behaviour to convince the world that you were the abusive one in the relationship.

His ability to harm you from a distance can sometimes be more frightening than when you were living with him. If he had a familiar routine or a deliberate pattern of abuse, you may have been comforted by the realisation that you knew what was about to happen, and that you had managed to survive his behaviour while you lived with him. When you no longer have regular contact with him, or when he can arrive into your life unexpectedly, you may find yourself more anxious and helpless than when you were together. Until he can no longer reach you physically or emotionally, you are in danger and should stay on your guard.

19. Surround yourself with proper support

The good intentions of others can leave you feeling more alone

One of the constant themes raised by my clients is the fear of being lonely and alone. This fear may be the result of his constant control: you might convince yourself that you could not manage without his presence. After years of intimate control, you may have become institutionalised and withdrawn. This reliance on the structure that he has created, and the prison in which you live, might make you afraid to step outside, into the freedom that you deserve. You may also be in touch with friends, family or advisers who want you to break out of your jail because they are sad to see you suffer. These people know that you deserve to be treated with respect and dignity, but are aware that your partner treats you with distain. It is hard for them to witness this treatment, and they want it to end quickly. Like some of my clients, you may have reached a point where all you advisers are telling you to leave your relationship and are constantly giving you new information about your partner. Your therapist may become critical of your lack of progress. The media may have informed you that no woman should stay with a psychephile. Many people will want what is best for you, but they may also believe that they know what is best for you.

You may have arrived at a stage where the desire for freedom, the effects of being institutionalised and the conflicting messages from your supporters have left you with a sense of anxiety and confusion. These effects are compounded by your partner, who will threaten you and misinform you. He may add to your anxiety by letting you know that he has many tactics of intimidation and control that he has not yet used. He may try to convince you that you have little or no legal standing, and that he will win any legal battle. He may also attempt to persuade you that he would have the children live with him, and that they would condemn you for the breakup of the family.

You may find yourself unable to think for yourself because of all the conflicting messages you are getting. You may also find that the more you talk to your partner, and to your friends, about your future, the greater your fear and sense of confusion become. You may become aware that you have been very alone for most of your relationship, and that even the people who have been helpful towards you have not understood you or the experiences you have endured.

Help can restore your confidence

It might be helpful if you could find some friends who will encourage you to listen to your own voice. You may be out of touch with your clear thinking, and may no longer trust your instinct, but any solution to your dilemma that comes from within your own psyche will be much more accurate, and also easier to implement, than the 'good advice' of well-intentioned friends. You might begin this process by taking a break from talking about him, and by encouraging your friends to stop mentioning him to you. This exercise can be time-limited: you could promise yourself that you will not discuss him for a number of weeks or even months. If you begin this process, you will quickly realise (a) how much he dominated your conversations, (b) how unhelpful it has been to talk about him because he hasn't changed, and (c) what a relief it is to talk about something more interesting than his behaviour.

If you commit to this experiment with your friends, you will quickly identify the ones who can be helpful to you. These friends will be the ones who listen to your request and respect your wish, even if they do not think it is a good idea. Your unhelpful friends may ignore your request and continue to introduce your abuser's name into your conversations. They may go so far as to criticise your decision and advise you that you must talk about your problems. Some of your so-called friends may also want to talk about your problems when you are not there, and criticise your indecisiveness. These are the friends who believe that they know better than you.

Two good friends are all you need

It may be that you are afraid that you may lose your friends if you do not accommodate their suggestions. It would be very helpful for you to avoid the people who make you fearful. You have lived a lifetime of anxiety with your partner, and do not need people in your life who make you feel anxious in their company. You will be very lucky if you can count on more than two really good friends. These are the people who respect your decisions and do not try to direct you into actions before you are ready to take these actions. They are the people who can quickly accept your need to free up your conversation, and will allow you to talk to them about a non-abusive future. They will be helpful without wanting to be compensated, they will listen without demanding that you listen to them, and they will surround you with encouragement and hope. They will be the very opposite of your abuser, and will help you experience the affection and appreciation you have been denied.

If you take a period of time when you avoid talking about him, you may find that your conversations with your friends become helpful and even humorous. In your controlled life, where your conversation is dominated by him, you may notice that you have lost your sense of humour; you may also be aware that your topics go round and round without making any progress. What will be of benefit to you is the knowledge that you are not required to keep him in the centre of your thoughts, and that it is possible for you to be distracted by other, more helpful topics. This possibility is worth exploring, because the more you do it, the more you regain control of your thoughts. You will begin to clear a small space in your mind; the light that might shine through that space could help lift the clouds of confusion that he has created. As the clouds lift, you may begin to see some options for your own future. When you are with your friends, you may begin to reveal the thoughts that you have about yourself, or you may hide some of your dreams and keep them secret.

You are entitled to have secrets

It would be better if you kept these options to yourself or your closest friend. If you have been abused for a long time, it might be useful to take some time to examine these options in the secrecy of your own heart. When you have examined them, it may be helpful to bring them to the attention of any person who will not criticise your thinking, and who will give you all the time you need to arrive at your own decision. You may decide to do nothing, or you may decide to get legal protection; you may decide to give him another chance, or you may visit a solicitor; you may decide to get help to cope, or demand that he gets some help. If your friend is good for you, he or she will give you space to examine the consequences of any decision you are planning to make.

Staying away

If you want to separate from him but feel obliged to keep some contact for the sake of your children, he may use that contact to intimidate you. Though most professionals are unclear on the issue, I believe that any man who abuses a child's mother cannot be regarded as a good parent. It would be very useful if you could get someone to act as a buffer between him and you regarding access to your children. You may be able to surround yourself with friends, family or other women in your position who would act as a contact during access. Many children are traumatised when they witness their mother being abused during the handover processes. Many fathers use access to abuse the mother further, and may lose interest in the process if they cannot use it to further traumatise her. Keep your children from being used as ammunition by staying out of the access process. You cannot be forced to liaise with or meet with your abuser. Some of my clients have been directed by the judiciary into facilitating access, attending mediation with the psychephile and developing a joint parenting plan. These instructions are a clear indication of the lack of awareness of the judiciary and the ability of your partner to 'groom' the judicial system. If you never meet him again, if you avoid his phone calls, if you ignore his texts, you will not miss any information that is intended for your benefit.

If you no longer share the same house, you may begin to realise that you have been alone for a long time. You may notice that being on your own is no worse, and hopefully much better, than sharing a home with a psychephile. When you are no longer in contact with your abuser, you may learn that being alone is better than sharing your life with a man who thinks you are not a person. You will eventually begin to wonder why, and how, you put up with his abuse for so long.

When you no longer wish to be part of his game, and no longer care if he is being 'good' or 'bad', you can begin to make your life an abuser-free zone. You can go through your day without mentioning his name. You can also avoid having people talk to you about him. Because he has accessed your mind by his use of language, it will be helpful if he is no longer part of your conversation. It can also be helpful if you refrain from discussing your partner with your children. I recommend that your home become a refuge for your family when he is not present. Talking about him with your children can also make him dominate their daily routines. This domination can undermine the joy of childhood for your children. When your children are encouraged to reduce their level of thinking about their father, when they are allowed to free their thoughts from the anxieties of being controlled and of being forced to take sides, they can give more space to their learning and imagination. It is very sad to hear my clients tell me that their children are grown up before they need to be. This development is best demonstrated by a five-year-old girl I know who saw her father assault her mother and subsequently asked her mother, 'Why did you marry him?' I believe that no five-year-old child should have to ask such a question.

When you establish a new home, you should make it a place of refuge for your mind. You should avoid mental contamination by not allowing his voice to invade your sanctuary.

20. Be proud of your survival
His mind-control is extensive

Anyone who has been the target of brainwashing techniques can find it difficult to survive the experience, and recover from it. But most of these targets are only recipients of these techniques for a limited amount of time. Most political prisoners and cult recruits are subjected to mind-control techniques for several years. In these cases, the bombardment of the target's thoughts is made difficult because the abuser does not know what the target is really thinking. Some religious cults gain occasional access to these innermost thoughts by the use of confession. But these situations are usually contrived, and are unable to assess whether the penitent is telling the truth.

The context of an intimate relationship allows your abuser to have access to your innermost thoughts and fears. He uses this information to sharpen his tactics and to target the very issues that are of value to you. This kind of informed mind-control is much more powerful than that experienced in non-intimate relationships.

The context of intimacy is unique: you have probably told your partner of experiences that you have had and dreams that you carry, which you have not told anyone else about. The psychephile learns your secrets and turns that information into ammunition against you. This level of access is unique to the context of an intimate relationship and is part of the reason why intimate abuse and violence does not fit on the continuum of stranger violence. This level of access also explains why good intentions and misinformed interventions have had little impact on the lives of male intimate abusers.

He knows more about you than any other person

He knows what you think, he knows what you hope for and he knows what upsets you. He also knows what confuses you and what makes you anxious. He has learned the triggers that make you feel afraid and he knows how to make you angry. He can use your good nature to make you feel guilty, and he can join in with others who make you feel inadequate. He has unique access to your spirit and unique knowledge of what motivates you. This insider information is stored by your abuser and may not be used immediately against you. You have probably been amazed when he brought up some issue about you that you had thought had been forgotten. This tactic of using your inner world against you can be frightening: you begin to wonder what else he remembers about your earlier conversations.

His accumulated knowledge of you and your way of thinking will cause you to wonder if he knows everything about you, and may allow him to persuade you that he remembers details about you that you have forgotten. You will be more upset because he will exaggerate and lie about the things he already knows, and challenge you to accept his version of the past. These lies and

135

exaggerations are only possible in the context of an intimate relationship. They are extremely powerful, as they dismantle your own personal protection and leave you emotionally vulnerable to him. He is the only person who can make you feel frightened and unhappy on a permanent basis. He is the only person who lies to you, and about you, on a permanent basis. He is the only person who regulates your emotions, as he has invaded your inner world.

He uses knowledge of your humanity to de-humanise you

It is unfortunate, but this man is the person that you want to love and nurture. He is the man whom you serve in so many ways, without any appreciation. He is the man who you have sex with when it suits him. He may be the father of your children and may even be a good provider, but he has no respect for you, and denies you the right of negotiation. He is so well informed that you may begin to think that he knows you better than you know yourself. He is so alert to your emotional life that he can tell you what you are feeling, and maybe what you are thinking, without you telling him. You may begin to believe that he can see into your spirit and read your mind. This lack of privacy, this sense of naked vulnerability, strips you of your dignity, your femininity and your humanity.

He wants to objectify you and regards you as an object that he owns

It takes extraordinary depth of character to remain sane while subjected to inti-mate mind-control, and it takes an extraordinary amount of strength and kind-ness to keep going in the face of such abuse. You may be angry with yourself because you still have feelings for this man, and retain some hope that he will improve. This false hope is also generated by him. Once he has gained access to your mind, he can feed any sort of information to you in a way that he knows will have an impact. He can also generate anxiety, confusion, fear and despair when it suits him. He is convinced that he can erode your core beliefs about yourself and then dictate to you how you should live your life as an attachment to him. You become his possession.

An emotional war-zone

Your psychephile has waged a focused and skilled attack on your spirit; as a result, you have been living on a rollercoaster of emotions for years. You have no refuge and are seldom at peace. Your home, which should be your haven, is contaminated with his influence, and he has a permanent presence in your psy-che. You may be ill with headaches or stomach pains, and treat these illnesses as symptoms of your weakness. You may even attend doctors and consultants, who believe your sickness is self-inflicted because you are ashamed to let them know of your abusive partner. While most people have stresses in their lives, you are in a unique situation in that you share a bed with the source of your stress. If your doctor knew that you were sharing a bed with the source of your contamination, they would encourage you to avoid that bed. If your cardiac consultant knew that your heart was broken, she would want you to avoid further injury. If your psychologist or therapist knew that your mind had been invaded, she would put a barrier up to any further invasion.

Everyone wants you to cope with the abuse or to run away

Sadly, your symptoms are diagnosed as being caused by yourself. Even the most well-intentioned people want you to protect yourself. Some of them may even want you to acknowledge that you draw much of your unease on yourself. You will be advised how to manage your pain and diminish your emotional bleeding. You will be misunderstood, criticised and even blamed by your supporters, because they do not know what a psychephile does.

You may begin to realise that you are very much alone, and that most of the encouragement you get makes you feel even more inadequate. People will want to empower you, when it is their duty to protect you. If you were left alone, if your partner could no longer get at you, you would manage your own world very well, and would grow in confidence as you regained control of your thinking. You will probably never encounter a more difficult problem than your life with a psychephile. As you are reading this, you might like to congratulate yourself because, in spite of his best efforts, you have a hidden strength which he has failed to conquer. Your integrity, your sense of fairness, your respect for others, your ability to commit to what is right, your willingness to apologise, and your stamina are aspects of your character which will help you flourish, once you stop wasting them on your abuser. I am convinced that any woman who, like you, can survive the mental cruelty that you have experienced, is well capable of living a worthwhile life.

Appreciation

As a result of your good nature, you are probably aware that you do things for people who take your kindness for granted. It is unlikely that all your children appreciate you all the time, but it is the role of every parent to act with care and attention until such time as they become young adults. But outside of your children, your responsibility extends equally to yourself and others. As a guiding principle, I would suggest that you only do things for people who appreciate you. My clients tell me that while this rule is difficult to instigate, it is amazing how much energy they have in areas where they are appreciated. Put yourself first, so that you will be better able to serve those whom you love.

While the psychephile has access to your thoughts, you will remain a victim to his malevolence: when you no longer encounter him, you become a survivor.

These words are very inadequate labels for who you really are. As the psychephile is still in your life, I am certain that you are a kind and decent woman who is loyal and dedicated to your family. I hope that you may arrive at a view of yourself which no longer includes the experience of being brainwashed. The psychephile is the one who is less than human, and he is the one who needs diagnosis and help. You deserve to be reminded that you have remained true to your principles of humanity and decency. If you can, I would invite you to begin to recall the things you do in a way that restores your belief and pride in yourself. You have had very little acknowledgement or praise since you met your abuser, but you can begin to redress the balance by reminding yourself of the little things you do well. If it would be helpful, you might dare to put a sign on your fridge door that reminds you that you are an awesome human being, a loyal partner and a dedicated mother.

Summary

Self-priority

Put yourself first

- Because you are kind, you may not remember a time when you were allowed to put yourself first.
- Try to reserve your kindness for those who appreciate you.

Clarify your options

- When you believe that you have no role to play in your abuse, you can begin to see your options.
- As your instinct becomes clearer, you will be able to make valid choices.

Stay alert and afraid

- Your emotional health can be damaged by him, even when he does not live with you.
- If he has access to you through your children, he can bombard you with messages about your children.

Surround yourself with proper support

- Your abuser can groom anyone who tries to help you.
- Find people who will help to protect your spirit and allow you to be yourself.

Be proud of your survival

- It takes extraordinary emotional strength to survive being intimate with someone who wants to de-humanise you.
- Appreciate yourself as doing so will increase your energy and encourage you to make a good life for yourself.

Part 3

Chapter Ten

Practical Advice and Options

As mentioned in the previous chapter, I would like to invite you to explore some options for your future. Please remember that you can reject or ignore my list of possibilities, as I am not an expert on your life. You have all the talent and wisdom to make a good life for yourself and your family, and you are by far the best judge of what will work in your particular circumstances. The work that I do is blessed by my observing the slow and effective development of my client's change of attitude and belief. Sadly, some of my clients do not have the luxury of time.

How can you handle being at high risk?

You may be in a situation of high risk, and need immediate protection. Sometimes you may want to minimise that risk and pretend that even though you have been threatened with serious injury or death, the psychephile would never commit such a serious crime. You may have gone to the community for protection and been ignored. You may have been offered forceful help, like being moved to a refuge or having him barred from your home, and rejected this approach as being too severe. You may be prepared to suffer on for the sake of the family, but be unaware of the risk and damage to your children this approach may bring. If you want to, or are advised to take immediate steps to secure the safety of your family, please do so without letting your abuser know what you are planning. If you ignore the help that is offered, you may be held accountable by your friends or advisers for the suffering of your children, even though you are not the abuser.

The high risk to you and your family may be recognised by professionals if some dangerous factors are present. Some psychephiles act above the law and ignore court orders. This contempt for the legal system will allow the abuser to believe that he is invincible, and that he will not tolerate any sanction. If the man has assaulted you with any kind of weapon, he may increase his use of this weapon, or he may get a more forceful weapon. This process may intensify until he uses a lethal weapon, such as a knife, hammer or gun. He may also develop a tendency of holding you by your throat, which can develop into fatal strangulation. These obvious assaults are an indication that your abuser has no interest in your well-being. Instead, they are an indication that you are worthless, and that the only reason he does not kill you is his fear that he might be caught. A number of my clients are dead because I ignored the warning signs. If the psychephile becomes convinced that he can get away with a lethal assault, he may kill his partner, and feel justified in doing so.

If you are living in a situation where your intuition is telling you that you must escape, then it is best if you do so quietly. Do not threaten to leave: he will not want you to go. I strongly advise you to contact a women's shelter, or the police, before you make any changes, or have a trusted friend do this for you. Find out what they advise women in your position to do. There are many webpages and telephone hotlines you can look up to find information about the safest possible means of escape. At all times, please be aware that it is better that your gut feeling of being in danger is taken seriously on time too many, than the other way around. Be cautious to the verge of silliness. Do not surf the internet for information if you have the slightest reason to believe that your partner can follow your digital tracks. Do not call numbers that end up on the phone bill, as he may see them. All these safety measures are vital to your safety and well-being. Above all, please do not ignore the risk you are in.

Do not threaten to tell the police, because he may be ready to groom them. Do not give any prior notice to your children, as one of them may be on his side and reveal your plans to him. Your partner may also put your children under pressure to reveal any secrets about you. It would be healthier for your children if they were not privy to any of your secrets. You may not want to leave your family home, and instead you might make full use of the protection of the courts. Many of our clients have found the response of the police to be very good, and to give a high level of protection to them. You may have that experience, but you might also be treated with distain by some members of the police. This may not be deliberate on their part, but an indication of the level of tolerance that exists towards intimate abuse. This tolerance is added to by the tendency of the community to blame you for your own misfortune. The officer assigned to your case may be a man who believes that giving priority to men is acceptable, or she may be a woman who believes that some women deserve to be abused. Either way, the response you get from the police can vary; your partner knows that he can groom most officers. Most national police in Western Europe carry guidance on their websites for women who are at risk, or will refer you to supportive organisations. If you are unsure whether you will be trusted, you can always make a phone call anonymously. Call back later if you do not get to talk to a supportive person; there are supportive people everywhere. Do not give up hope. You are worthy of protection. You are worthy of living safely.

The legislation on intimate abuse is regularly updated in most countries. The grounds for getting a barring or safety order are changed to reflect the changing shape of relationships. The services available to women are being streamlined, and the child agency protection services are developing practices and procedures which might be more effective in protecting you and your children than those that exist at present. But, sadly, all these improvements do not tackle the core problem, which is the behaviour of your partner. Like most psychephiles, your partner believes he is above the law. He may also be aware of how the law is changing, and respond accordingly. The reason why the protection of the law is not consistent is that your psychephile is accepted by society and his rights are, some would argue, given preference over yours. Your abuser is more dangerous than most paedophiles as he is more talented at setting up and grooming, yet because you are an adult, his behaviour is minimised, and you are blamed for upsetting him or not understanding his needs.

Before you consider your long-term options, you need to consider one more thing, which seems to contradict what I have just been looking at. You need to remind yourself that, in a sense, you are very much alone. The community sees you as a problem to be solved. It may not be possible for you to convince them that the real problem is the behaviour of your partner. Get ready for this attitude, because it will prepare you for what is to come, and increase your resilience when you are questioned.

You may have already planned different ways of escape. As I already suggested, it would be helpful to think about your own safety first and to assess any plan in terms of how it would benefit you. Try not to think of the reaction of your abuser, as his behaviour when you leave is seldom predictable. In many cases, he can become more dangerous, so it is best to plan for severe intimidation and even serious assault when he realises that you are leaving or that you have moved out. He is very likely to bombard you with complaints and instructions, and to threaten you with increased violence. If you ask friends and family for advice, bear in mind that they are unlikely to grasp the degree danger you are in. Certainly, it is highly unlikely that they will see the danger in the form of thought-control. They may find it hard to grasp the terror you face, and it will be even harder for them to grasp the terror that may follow. By all means, hang on to family and friends you trust, but take advice and counsel about the actual leaving from those with long and proven experience in this area, such as women's shelters or special units in the police. If you are unable to find such a unit locally, look for one in the nearest city to you.

You may initially feel that you have made the wrong move, and believe that you could have had more influence over him if you had stayed with him. Some of my clients even try to influence and plead with their abuser after they have moved out. This negotiation is seldom productive, as the abuser is less likely to cooperate with you when you have left him. Abused women have insisted on remaining in contact with their abusers while staying in a refuge or safe house, in the belief that they need to know what he is planning. This contact is very damaging: the psychephile will lie to you about the reality of his life and will threaten or seduce you in an attempt to get you to come back to him. While he has access to your thoughts, he will be able to invade your spirit and he will confuse and frighten you. He can do this directly, through face-to-face contact, or by phone, text or email. He can also do it through other people, including your children, family and friends. Some abusers make updates on social media with a message only you can understand. He might also have friends who collude with him and make such posts. If he fails to get you to comply with his wishes, he will begin to use solicitors and courts to keep his place in your thoughts. The aim is to make sure he is constantly at the centre of your attention, to make you silent and scared, and eventually to wear you down, until you are ruined. Never believe that he does all this in order to have you back because you are a human of value to him. If you have a value, it is measured by other standards. He will use whatever tactic works: even though you may not see him for weeks or months, he can still dominate your thoughts and dictate the state of your emotional health.

While you are at high risk, it would be helpful if you allowed the community to protect you and your children. Moving to a refuge, going to stay for a while with family or friends, having an adult come and live in your home, or getting a dog or a secure house are some of the ways my clients have obtained temporary safety. Using court orders, safety orders or barring orders or other injunctions can be useful, in that they give the police greater powers to act quickly and effectively.

If you do get a court order, I would encourage you to use it. Do not be afraid to report every breach of the order to your local police station. I would encourage you to get the officer to take a statement each time you report an incident, and to demand a signed copy of each statement. These statements can be used in court if you need to pursue a case. It can be useful to be accompanied by a friend when visiting a police station, because if you are alone you may not always get the cooperation you deserve. Some of my clients have been abused or dismissed by the police, and you may find that tolerance and blame are common within the force.

The court system does not understand how a psychephile operates, and solicitors can be groomed by them. If you go to court and your abuser is represented by a solicitor, you will probably be surprised when you hear lies and distortions presented to the court as if they were fact. The solicitor is only repeating what your abuser said, and has no way of verifying the truth of any statement. The court is confused by the conflicting evidence presented by you and your abuser. It might be of benefit to you if you avoided the back-and-forth exchanges which usually occur when you are seeking a court order. As the judge may not know more than the bare details of your case, he or she may be seduced by your abuser. Every psychephile is an expert in lying to make himself look good, and are often good at gaining sympathy from the judge. Some judges can be made to feel pity for the man, especially if he or she believes that 'marriage is all kicks and kisses' (district court judge, Cork, 2002). This judge, and others, may also believe in male sexual priority, and that the concept of implied consent applies in intimate relationships.

Some of my clients have successfully adopted a different approach when they have been asked to speak in court. They have refused to get into arguments with the abuser or his solicitor. They have declared that they have no wish to castigate their partner but that they want the court to know that they are terrified of their spouse and are seeking the protection of the court for the future. I have advised some of my clients to repeat this position as often as needed, and to maintain a dignified silence when being badgered by the other side. If you do this, you will feel that you did not let yourself down: even if you do not get what you had hoped for, you will know that you did your best. It can be very reassuring if you emerge from the courts with your sense of self enhanced. It will be very frustrating for your abuser if he fails to manipulate you in the courts.

It is good to remember that you are not as convincing as your abuser when you argue with him. He can twist the truth, enhance his image, exaggerate your weaknesses and can denigrate your talents, so that you appear to be the cause of all the distress in the relationship. You may have heard most of these statements before, but many of my clients have been alarmed to hear that their spouses use new lies before the courts. This practice of lying to the court is a crime (perjury), but it is unlikely that the court will have time to charge your abuser with this crime. I have personally, or in reports from target women and professionals, heard men make the most outrageous statements without them being challenged. This gives every psychephile the feeling that he is above the law and can say what he likes in court.

Another issue which is prevalent in the courts is the reluctance of the legal system to treat family abuse as criminal matter. When you go for a court order, you go to the family court, which is a civil court. When there is evidence that a court order has been breached, the issue moves to the criminal court. Even if the case is proven in the criminal court, the judge is unlikely to issue a custodial sentence. Most women who are being abused do not engage in the court system, and as a result many abusers believe that nothing will happen to them. They think they will get away with their bad behaviour because they believe they can manipulate the court system.

Can you be fair to someone who is unfair?

The court system is designed to apply the law in a just and fair way. The judge can only deal with evidence that is verifiable, but in family law there is usually an amount of hearsay evidence presented. This means that you may tell the court some of the things that happened to you. Your abuser may deny these accusations, or he may ignore your evidence and make exaggerated claims about your bad behaviour. He may even make false claims about you, including that you have been unfaithful, that you have a drink problem, that you have spent all his money, and that you are a very poor parent. These lies are presented to the court as though they are true because of the skill of your abuser in grooming his own legal team.

Your abuser also knows that these claims can really upset you. He believes that, if you are angry in the courtroom, you will lose favour with the judge. He is extremely anxious to make you upset: he knows he can manipulate your reaction once he can get you to listen to him. You may want to be fair to him and not mention the details of his bad behaviour. You may not tell the judge of his persistent degradation of you, his constant manipulativeness, his invasion of your spirit, and his sexual dominance of you. You may not want him to be punished for his previous crimes, though you want the court to protect you from further abuse.

Your abuser wants to win. He believes that he is entitled to do so, but he is also arrogant enough to believe that if he can upset you before the courts, the judge will be lenient with him. He lacks any notion of fairness: he is convinced that you do not deserve to be treated like a woman. He believes that his sexual partner is not a human being but, rather, an object that is there to be exploited. He has exploited you throughout the relationship and will continue to treat you as an object rather than a person.

It may be naive to go into court with a belief that you can be fair to him, and that he will appreciate your fairness and treat you as you deserve to be treated. If you go before a judge, I would recommend that you go there to get some safety for yourself. Do not expect your abuser to cooperate with you, your own legal team to be fair to you, the judge to recognise the lies that the abuser presents to the court, and your abuser to abide by any agreement that is put in place by the judge. You should consider telling the judge that you do not want any punishment for him but that you do want protection for yourself and your children.

Do the courts understand these men?

Few judges have been trained to recognise the grooming tactics that every psychephile uses in the courts, and it would appear that very few solicitors and barristers are prepared to challenge the lies that these psychephiles use. These men can manage to get the courts to accept their explanations and excuses. I have encountered some psychephiles who have managed to get court officials to feel sorry for them. I know of psychephiles who have burst into tears in court in order to get the judge on their side. One of my clients was astonished when her husband arrived into the courtroom on crutches; the judge complimented him for making a great effort to be present. The same woman was scared when her husband then told the judge that he had met his wife's lover (she did not have one), that there had been a tussle, and that this man had broken his ankle. The judge was so taken by the man's plight that he wanted to adjourn proceedings until the man was in better health. My client said that she had no objection to an adjournment but would insist that the man who was supposed to be her lover be identified to the court before the next hearing. When the man on crutches heard this, he decided that he was well enough to proceed on the day.

It is unlikely that the solicitors or judges learned anything from this incident, and that they continued to be manipulated into colluding with psychephiles. The courts tend to see these men as good husbands and partners who occasionally lose their tempers. They do not show any interest in the pattern of targeting, setting up and grooming that is used by all psychephiles. The courts fail to acknowledge that these tactics are similar to those used by paedophiles. What is even less well understood is the fact that a man who wants to groom an adult needs to be more skilful and more persistent than a paedophile, because the target is an adult and the psychephile wants the relationship to last. Very few men or women understand what drives a psychephile to want to sexually dominate a woman who wants to love him; only women who have lived with a psychephile have a good understanding of what these men are like. But even the target-woman herself does not understand who he really is and why he behaves so badly.

No matter how long you try to figure out who your abuser is, you will be unable to draw any conclusions, because you do not know him. You may have shared his bed for years, reared his children and comforted him when times were tough, but he still remains hidden from you. All psychephiles hide their real selves and present a facade of who they really are. They may appear to be kind and sympathetic when it suits them, and as a result many people are unaware of their nasty side. Your friends may have already witnessed how he treats you in their company, however, and may be so upset by it that they now avoid being in his company. While these friends see his bad behaviour, they are unable to understand it, and so you may find that they stay away from your home. These men are skilled in hiding their real agenda. They do not want anyone to diagnose their intentions or behaviours. The judges and solicitors do not understand him, because they are not trained to look behind the facade of his lies. They are unable to realise how intense and persistent his abuse is, because nobody has taken the time to draw an accurate diagnosis of him.

Do the courts want to sanction them?

It is unlikely that a psychephile will be sanctioned by the court system. Some abusive men who are not very skilled at manipulation – in other words, those who are not fully developed psychephiles – may have the sanction of a court order applied to them. The skilled offender may find a way of avoiding a court order being issued. If you go to court with a psychephile, you may find yourself withdrawing the application for a court order, or you may agree to accept a promise given to your solicitor. Though this promise is given within the court, it has little legal value and your partner will probably ignore it as soon as you drop the proceedings. Your solicitor may encourage you to accept this promise because he or she cannot believe that your abuser is so devious.

If you do obtain a court order, either a safety order or a barring order, it is important that you use the protection that you have been granted. Most orders will demand that your abuser does not frighten or intimidate you and your children. You can report any incident where your abuser threatens you or your children. If you have a barring order, you can report any time your partner tries to enter your home. Your order may also prohibit him from approaching you on the street, at the children's school, or at your place of work.

If your abuser breaches a court order – in other words, if he ignores the instructions of a judge – he can be arrested immediately. This can happen because the court order gives more authority to the police and allows them to act in what is now regarded as a criminal matter. It can also happen because a psychephile who thinks he can avoid being sanctioned when there is an order in place, is a high-risk abuser. You may not want to see your partner arrested, and you may not want to have your children upset by knowing that the police have taken their father away. This kindness and attitude can be harmful for both your children and your abuser.

One of my clients went to her local district court to get a barring order, but the judge refused her, saying that her children would be traumatised. The same judge came to my office a year later with a request that I give an appointment to his daughter, who had been assaulted by her partner the previous day. I asked him if his daughter was at risk of further abuse; the judge told me that he had contacted the partner and instructed him to leave the house and never return. This judge had barred the assailant because he realised that the target-woman needed to be protected. Any of my clients who applied for court protection after that event were usually granted what they asked for by this judge.

Your children are aware that you have been abused, ignored and degraded over a period of many years. They also know that their father gets away with bad behaviour and that he uses fear to get his way. They are witnesses to some of the abuse, and may have been abused themselves. Many of them will get caught up in the war, and may even try to regulate it. Some of them may also be groomed into taking sides, and may even be used as weapons. If they grow up and leave home while the abuse continues, they may believe that such a relationship is normal and that loving relationships are impossible.

Any kindness to your abuser on your part is misplaced. He has gone through life believing in his own entitlement. The more he gets his own way, the more he grooms people into colluding with him, and the greater his arrogance becomes. Your kindness is never appreciated. Instead, it feeds his selfishness until he swells up with his own importance. Eventually he puts himself on a pedestal, where he believes he is above the law. Unless he gets a strong message that he is not, he may die believing that he is a little god.

Can you mediate with a liar?

Mediation is usually a process where you and your abuser sit down with a third party and try to repair your relationship (relationship counselling) or work out a separation agreement in an amicable way. You may attend these meetings in the belief that the mediator will be fair to both of you. You may also hope that your abuser will be honest and tell the truth about his abuse. You will probably be very nervous going into these meetings, because your intuition will be telling you that he will not change. Your gut will be telling you that he will try to groom the mediator; you know that he is very good at getting people to take his side. You may even have tried to get family or friends to mediate for you in the past, and discovered that he could win them over.

If you look back over the course of your relationship with him, you will realise that you could never negotiate an agreement with him, even about small things. You will remember that, if you wanted to do something, he only went along with your wishes when it suited him to do so. You will have noticed that, if he wanted to do something which you did not agree with, he seldom changed his mind, even if you pleaded with him. Over the course of the relationship, your partner may discuss issues with you when he already knows that he is going to win. If he cannot win the argument by persuasion, he may become aggressive and intimidating. If he is unable to overcome your resistance, he may become abusive or violent.

When you look back over these discussions, you may begin to realise that his statements are littered with exaggerations and lies. You will notice that he will deny any anxiety that you may feel. He will want you to accept that he is always right and that, if something did not work out on a previous occasion, he was not to blame. He wants to persuade you that you were to blame for the out-come – or, if you were not to blame, then some other stupid person was at fault.

You may also have experienced the use of the 'silent' tactic, where your abuser fails to convince you that he is right about a certain issue, and may stop talking to you. Some psychephiles can maintain this silence for months, until you eventually give in to him, or until the issue is no longer a concern on his part. If you have been subjected to this tactic, you may have found it easier to agree with him than to live with the strain of a prolonged silence. If you are living with a psychephile, you will quickly learn that he believes that he is seldom wrong, and that he will never concede to your opinion.

Going into mediation with such a man is not only ineffective but may be dangerous for you. Because you expect that the mediator will not allow him to become aggressive, you may have some hope that he will respect the mediator and cooperate with the process. This is unlikely to happen. The psychephile knows that aggression and intimidation may not work in his favour, so he uses a different set of tactics. He sets out to charm the mediator with half-truths and lies. He will present himself as good and will describe you as the problem. He will lie about his concern for his children and about your ability to be a good parent. He will lie about the amount of money he has, or about your spendthrift habits. If he goes to the pub regularly, he will lie about the frequency of such visits, and about the amount of alcohol he consumes. If you drink alcohol, he will lie about the amount you consume, and about the effects of your drinking on the whole family. You may be accused of being a flirt, or of having an affair, even though there is no evidence of this. He will use these lies and exaggerations to win the sympathy of the mediator, in the belief that if the mediator feels sorry for him, he may get what he wants out of the process.

One of the other damaging effects of mediating with a psychephile is the danger that you will give him information about your negotiating position. This information will allow him to draw you into a process where you will begin to give in to him in various areas. He has learned over the years that you can be manipulated, and he will use all his guile to get you to give way on certain things that are of benefit to him. If you have been unable to negotiate successfully with your abuser during the relationship, it is unlikely that you will be able to do so successfully when he realises that the relationship is over.

My recommendation to you would be that you avoid any situation where you will be subjected to more of his manipulation and lies. You might be obliged by your legal team, or by a judge, to attend mediation, as it is recommended by most legal practitioners. If you go to meet a mediator, I would suggest that you alert the mediator to the possibility that your partner may tell lies. I would like you to make it very clear that you will withdraw from the meeting if your abuser begins to lie. This might seem a little dramatic, but it is your safeguard. If you allow the meeting to continue, you will begin to lose your ground, and the mediator will be seduced by his lies. You will never be able to compete with his lies, and you will not be able to get him to withdraw his statements.

Any of my clients who used this ultimatum did not stay at the meeting for more than ten minutes. They found that the abuser tried to groom the mediator by lying about his good behaviour and denigrating his partner's behaviour. As in every other company, the psychephile will want to be in control. He knows he can control you, but he must get the mediator to feel admiration or sympathy for him. You may find that he has already spoken to the mediator and has already started his grooming tactics.

One of my current clients has just discovered that the court-appointed mediator has already visited the family home from which she fled in terror, and has concluded that her ex-husband is a reasonable man and that my client is the one with the anger issues. Sadly, the mediator has already been groomed by the psychephile and has no idea of the fifteen years of intimidation, degradation, assault and evil that caused the client to flee with her young child. I encouraged my client to present a detailed history of the abuse she has endured (she kept a daily diary throughout her marriage) to the mediator, and then invite the mediator to tell her how she ought to feel.

The client decided to postpone the initial meeting with the mediator in her own home. She arranged to meet him at a neutral venue and indicated that she did not want to explore any solutions until the mediator was clear about the real problem. The mediator expressed shock at her story, and at the ability of her abuser to groom him. The client is now ready for the next step, and has invited the mediator to visit her in her home and to meet her child. I am fairly sure that if she had ignored the initial setup by her abuser, she would be compromised by the report, and would be let down by the recommendations of the court. I want her to be able to tell her child that she resisted playing the game that is being orchestrated by her ex-partner.

Try not to blame the mediator if he or she has been compromised. Your psychephile is far more devious than the mediator can accept. Remember what I have been saying throughout this book: the sole reason your partner is able to get his way is because his behaviour is incomprehensible by any normal standard, and the scientific community has yet to find the reasons for this. You will know that friends or family have already fallen for his lies, and that your abuser has never done anything that is for your benefit. You will hear the beginnings of an untruth which you have heard before, but you will not be able to convince the mediator that your abuser is lying. You may hear lies that you have never previously heard. You may be awestruck at how easily your abuser can relate false stories that go beyond his previous lies.

There is little point in you or any other target-woman being subjected to further lies, and there is no benefit for you in watching another person being manipulated by him. Being true to yourself means withdrawing from the session or sitting quietly until it is over. If you are drawn into defending yourself or challenging him, you will be sucked into his game – a game you cannot win. It is extremely encouraging if you can leave with dignity and leave him feeling unsure of himself, or even helpless. Like some of my clients, you may feel a sense of pride in yourself that you gave a public message that you would not allow yourself to be subjected to any more of his lies.

It is impossible to mediate with a liar, because he never exposes his real agenda. He wants to win, and this means that you must lose.

Chapter Eleven

Emotional Advice and Options

How can he switch so easily from being reasonable to being angry?

It is difficult to witness a man who is being reasonable suddenly change into an apparently angry abuser. Some of the psychephiles have done so in my office. Some of them have tried to seduce me into colluding with them by portraying themselves as being responsible and anxious. Others have tried to seduce me into feeling sorry for their frustration. I have also been invited to accept their assessment of their target-woman as the person who is the cause of their marital difficulties. When I decline to rush to judgement or to take sides as they wished, I can be threatened and intimidated. On one occasion, I was told by a psychephile who was about to leave my office in tears that he was going to kill himself and that he would leave a note to say that his death was my fault. His tears were designed to put pressure on me into feeling sorry for him, as he was going before a judge later that week to be charged with GBH (grievous bodily harm) because he had fired a shotgun at his wife and injured her leg. He wanted me to write to the judge and inform him that his wife, who was a client of mine, was a liar, and that she had staged the shooting so that she could have him barred from her home. What was apparent to me was that this man was an actor and a liar. Like all psychephiles, he was able to take on any role that might help turn things to his advantage, and was not emotionally engaged in any role. His tears and anger were fake; he could move from one position to another in an instant.

Another client described a night she had spent in her own home with her husband without getting any sleep. He had come home after midnight and wanted to have sex with her. She refused, and he began to rant at her. This continued throughout the night; at 7 am, she became so frightened that she ran from the house. Her husband was becoming increasingly angry, and she thought he was going to erupt. She forgot to pick up the keys of her car, and quietly opened the front door: her keys were on the hall-stand. She was amazed to hear her husband on the phone to one of his golfing partners, talking in a most polite and relaxed way about meeting up that morning. She could not believe that he could be so calm, after having been in a rage just a few minutes earlier.

If you or I had been in a rage and had been ranting at someone nonstop for more four hours, we would probably need to 'cool down' for a long time, before being able to communicate calmly again. This is because you or I would need to be emotionally very upset to express any sort of anger. We would require a huge level of emotional distress to sustain that anger for a few hours. This distress would eventually leave us drained.

Your abuser is not emotionally involved in appearing to be sad or in acting in an angry way. It is as easy for him to take on a particular role as it is for him to sleep. It does not use any of his emotional energy to maintain that role. Your abuser is never sad or angry. His energy is focused on deciding which role would be to his greatest advantage at any time. It is frightening to realise that each time he appeared to be angry with you, and you tried to soothe his upset, he was only acting, in order to get his own way. Do not be disappointed by your naivety: your abuser is a skilled operator who uses his talents to manipulate anyone he meets. When I recently heard a group of these men admit that they were never angry but could act angrily when it suited them I found that I was afraid of them.

We had good times

The abusive man who became your long-time intimate partner is not a fool. He knew that if he was to establish and maintain control over you, he would need to seduce and confuse you. During the seductive phase, he would have acted in ways that would convince you that he was the right man for you. He would have listened to your standards and principles concerning your intimate relationships, and he would want you to believe that he was the ideal man to measure up to those standards. He would have acted in a sympathetic way and demonstrated that he could be the ideal partner for you.

You may have cherished memories of times when you felt loved and appreciated. Your abuser knew that he needed to develop these memories and not fill your thoughts with anxiety at the beginning of your relationship. He knew that if he exposed his real intention at an early stage in your relationship, he might lose you. He covered his need to be in control and would not act on it initially. If he had been an unskilled abuser, he would have stymied your joy from an early stage by assaulting you or putting pressure on you to be sexually intimate (raping you). You may not wish to admit that you have been raped, but I believe that every time you have declined to be intimate but have subsequently conceded to his demands, you have suffered a rape.

The skill of your abuser is his ability to act in his own best interests at all times. This means that he needed to have constant access to your thinking and to avoid behaving in a way that would cause you to leave him. Your initial time together was designed by him to satisfy some of your desires. Some targets, upon hearing about the tactics of targeting, setting-up and grooming, recall hints at what would later become the rules of the abuse. He seemed to understand your need for love and affection. He acted as though he had respect for you, and that your love meant a great deal to him. He may have given you little gifts for what he would have described as your efforts to love him. He might have begun to speak about you in glowing terms to your friends. He might have told your family, and his family, how much you meant to him. Sometimes he might have embarrassed you with public displays of love and affection. You might have heard some of your friends say that he was a lovely guy and that you made a great couple. These were times when you felt joy and contentment. These feelings of being someone special mirror the feelings that a paedophile aims to generate in a young boy or girl.

It is a wonderful sensation when you believe that you are unique in someone's life, and you would have felt that you had been chosen because of your talents and your nature. This childlike feeling of satisfaction is warm and appealing. The memories linger for years, and you may find yourself returning to them long after the relationship changes. Without you knowing it, your abuser will remind you of these memories if he ever needs to re-groom you. The paedophile who needs to remain in contact with his target child will re-groom the child by reminding the child of the rewards they have already been given. Your intimate abuser will recall your good memories in an attempt to convince you that the good times in the relationship far outweigh the bad times.

This clever tactic leaves you confused and maybe even frustrated. You are confused because he is right when he says you had good times, and you are frustrated because you know he is capable of reproducing these good times in your relationship. What you may begin to realise is that the purpose of his good behaviour is not to make you feel emotionally content but to enhance your opinion of him. Like all good actors, he can behave like a wonderful lover and parent, and then can destroy all the good that he generates by changing his role to one of intimidation and demands. Yes you did have good times – because he knew that if you hadn't, you would have left him soon after you met him.

Did he ever love me?

This is a difficult question to answer in general terms, as the word 'love' means different things to different people. If you want to know if your abuser fancied you, or if you equate love with someone who pursues you, then your partner may have had those feelings for you. These feelings are described in male terms as lust. While such feelings are common for men, they are not connected with your feelings: he can lust after you without being concerned about your response. Young men who feel entitled to sex can persuade themselves that a woman is lusting for them even though the woman may have no such feelings.

If your partner is a psychephile it is unlikely he was ever fond of you in a way that would make you the centre of his world as you would have done for him. It is unlikely that you became his priority and he certainly did not support you in maintaining the world you lived in when you first met him. He probably introduced small changes in your routine gradually until you were spending most of your time in his world. This might have felt like love to you but it was not done in your best interest. You were never the centre of his world as he filled that role himself. You may check back over the relationship and see if your emotions were ever cared for. When you said you were sad or embarrassed did he show you that he cared for how you were feeling in a way that helped you? Or did he ignore your distress or tell you get over it? He probably went further and told you that your emotional discomfort was your own fault and that you were too naive or too sensitive for your own good.

If you ever experienced tenderness and affection with your partner, you may have believed that you were loved at those times. But if these emotions were generated so that he could seduce you, then your experience of love was conditional. You may have been told that he was devoted to you, or that he could not live without you, but this was probably just another act. When you look back over the whole of your relationship, you may find it hard to identify any act of his that was not driven by selfishness on his part. You may also find it hard to recall whether you were ever asked what you would like, and have him agree to your suggestion unless it suited him. If you asked him to go and visit your family, you may have been pleased when he said yes, but you were no doubt disappointed when he turned the visit into one of embarrassment or shame for you.

Though love is a useful aspect of a relationship, it needs to be founded on respect and appreciation. If these elements do not exist, it is probable that love will rapidly fade, and that the apparent acts of caring or affection will be hollow. If your partner was a skilled abuser when you met him, it is unlikely that he ever respected you. You will probably be able to recall small incidents in the early stages of the relationship when your opinion was ignored or rejected. You will remember when you expressed some important value in your life, only to be told that your belief was stupid or wrong. When you made an effort to calm the relationship, you were unlikely to be appreciated. It might be the case that even though you have been with the psychephile for years, you cannot recall ever feeling respected or appreciated.

Without these fundamental elements, all his apparently loving behaviour was driven by his own needs. If he did not respect you as a person, and did not acknowledge and appreciate the efforts you were making, he is unlikely ever to have loved you. It is also possible that he is incapable of loving any woman. Without an ability to respect you as a human being, he will have set out to de-humanise you and turn you into an object which he can possess. He will have done so in the guise of love. This behaviour can best be described as evil: the experience of many target women is certainly that they are living with an evil person.

Why do you still care?

When you were first targeted by your partner, he recognised that you were a kind person. He saw that you had a tendency to put the needs of others before your own. He learned this by listening to the way you spoke about others. If you were a selfish woman, he would have heard you talk mainly about yourself, and he would have noticed quickly that your world revolved around you. Such a woman would not be attractive to him in terms of a long-term relationship, though he may have had a series of short-term encounters until he met someone who would put him first in her world. He would only remain in a relationship with you when he knew that he could be the priority in your life. Many psychephiles have reassured me that they could recognise a 'kind target' within a short space of time, with some even claiming that they only needed half an hour to be certain that the target could be controlled.

This kindness that you have, this caring attitude that you have for other people, is what attracted your abuser to you in the first place. Your tendency to put the needs of others before yourself is a wonderful trait, and should not make you feel ashamed. Your abuser used this trait against you without you knowing it. He played on your kindness in the beginning, so that you went along with his wishes, even when you would have preferred to do something else. He played on your kindness when things between you were difficult, so that you took it upon yourself to calm the situation and to find ways of avoiding a repeat of the same difficulty. He also played on your kindness when he went too far in abusing you and then begged you for forgiveness.

The most powerful abuse of your kindness was when he began to get you to feel sorry for him. This feeling of pity is orchestrated by him so that you will carry a concern for him for a long time. He will present himself to you as helpless in some appealing ways, or he will regale you with false tales about his sad history. He may remind of the many injustices to which he has been subjected, and may even recount exaggerated tales of a deprived childhood. All these tactics will access your kind nature in a way that can diminish your spirit and overwhelm your instinctive defences. Your heart will be invaded with care and concern, because he wants you to feel these emotions. When he began to scare you, and went beyond your tolerance for his bad behaviour, when he ignored your pleading for better treatment, he ignored your requests and told you in some way that you did not care enough. If you stayed with him, you did so in the belief that if you cared more, your relationship would improve. The reason why you still care after years of abuse is because it is your nature to do so, and because your partner fostered that spirit in you through his manipulation and lies.

Was everything he said a lie?

When you first met your abuser, he was attracted by your tendency to be truthful. He encouraged this tendency by getting you to reveal things about yourself in an honest way. He may have even noticed how your mannerisms betrayed you if your tried to tell a lie. He could convince you that he knew you were not telling the truth, and he explained to you that one of the terms and conditions of your relationship was that you gave honest answers to his questions. This demand led you to strive to be more truthful, or to withdraw from some conversations. These conversations became difficult when he began to tell you that you were lying, when in fact you were telling the truth. He may have eventually persuaded you that he knew what you were thinking, and that he would continue to harangue you until you gave him the answer he wanted.

Being truthful also gave you a desire to believe others. You would accept his statements as being truthful, because you believed that you would know if he was lying. You were falling in love with this man, and you wanted to believe him, because you knew that the truth was important; you wanted to be in a relationship where the truth was valued. This desire to believe others is a healthy trait, but it was used in his favour by your partner. You may also have ignored some initial blatant lies he told you, in the belief that if you understood why he lied, you could eventually persuade him to tell the truth. You may even have told him that you would accept the truth, and would forgive him for whatever he had done that had caused him to lie. Looking back to the beginnings of your relationship, you may also remember a time when you felt that his lies were manageable and that, as part of your commitment to the relationship, you could ignore them and not let them undermine the good that you initially experienced from him.

Your abuser knew that you were having all these thoughts. He knew it because you told him that you were willing to subdue your concerns in the hope that he would make every effort to diminish his practice of deceiving you. You probably didn't make these commitments in any formal way, but in the intimacy of your conversations he monitored your willingness to ignore or to forgive. This monitoring allowed him to expand his untruths until it was possible for him to lie to you about anything. When he told you that you were a stupid woman, when he persuaded you that you were a bad mother, when he terrified you by convincing you that he could rape you when it suited him, he already knew that you would accept his lies. I am sure that if he had told you these lies when you first met him, you would have run away from the relationship. The skill of your psychephile is that he learned from your conversations how much of a lie you would accept from him. He also learned from your conversations that some lies had a greater impact on you than others.

It is unlikely that he ever told you the truth about anything of importance in your relationship. Everything he said may not have been completely untrue, but every revelation he made about you and your relationship was couched in language that was designed to confuse you and benefit him. Things may have gone so far that you now wonder whether he believed his own lies; you may appreciate that he lives in a parallel world where only his own rules apply.

Does he know what he is doing?

Many clients do not want to accept my answer to this question. You, and all other kind people, want to believe that no one could be so bad that they would want to invade the spirit of another, and that they would intentionally do so in a deliberate and skilful way. He is skilled because he can do so in a hidden way, and you will not know what he is really doing. He does so in a deliberate way without needing to devise a detailed plan. He has an instinctive ability to improve his own situation, and to use the world around him for his own advantage. He will have an exaggerated sense of entitlement which will override any sense of conscience he may have, and he will see nothing wrong in his behaviour. He believes that the end justifies the means, and that you have deserved all the abuse that you have suffered.

As he develops his control, and realises that he can avoid any sanction for his actions, he develops an arrogance which feeds on his success. He monitors his level of control, and carefully expands it until he is seldom resisted. He will meet any resistance with seduction, intimidation, threats or assaults. He will deliberately use only as much of these tactics as is needed to break down your resistance and put himself back in charge.

If you are already groomed to be afraid of him, you will be reluctant to uphold your resistance; he will know from previous events that he can wear you down.

He may degrade you with criticisms and foul language, or he may shut off communication and withdraw from you in silence. He may convince you that his lies are the truth, or that your stupidity makes you unable to see his reality. He will be focused and persistent, and may bombard you with his message, until your mind is full of him and your head feels as though it will explode.

Some time later, when he has achieved his victory, he will act as if nothing had happened, and convince you that your distress is caused by your own foolishness or sensitivity. He will resume his contact with the world around him, as though he did nothing wrong, and he will leave you to recover on your own. Sometimes, if he has overstepped one of your boundaries, he may offer a token apology so that you will not punish him.

All these behaviours are deliberate, but they are not planned in advance. He has the guile to be able to read relationship situations quickly and accurately. He does not spend time developing strategies, but does give some thought to the need for monitoring his progress. His strategies come from his ability to think fast, and his monitoring informs him of the limits he needs to apply to his actions. If he has already convinced you that he owns you in a sexual way, then he will deny you the right to your sexual integrity. If you indicate that you are denying him access to you sexually, you may be at much higher risk. Women who are murdered by their partners are usually killed when the man realises that his control is waning and what he sees as his sexual entitlement is being denied.

You may believe that he spends much time planning his next move, but this is unlikely. If your partner is abusive, he will have developed an intuitive – and successful – ability to manipulate the world around him, and to use it to satisfy his own needs. His selfishness dominates his thinking, and his deviousness allows him to follow his own desires without much restraint. He is always in control, and his actions are always deliberate. He may appear to be drunk or enraged, but he behaves in a deliberate and managed way. This fact, revealed to me by the groups of men with whom I originally worked, was the most unbelievable and frightening aspect of all of my early learning. Your psychephile has never abused you without knowing precisely what he was doing, and without being certain that he would achieve whatever he wanted. Knowing your intimate thoughts, he confidently intimidated and assaulted you using his most efficient tactics; usually achieved exactly what he wanted. If you reflect on your most frightening experiences, you will realise that your psychephile always won, and that you reacted in a way that suited him. A psychephile is always in control.

How does he control your children?

If you have children and are like most of my clients, you will want to believe that you can protect your children from being intimidated by and afraid of their father. You may even believe that your children do not know of the abuse you are experiencing. You will be anxious that your children will grow up to be decent adults; you hope that they will not repeat the behaviour of their father or the experience of their mother.

It becomes difficult to accept that the father of your children is always seeking ways to control those around him. He can be very cooperative when it suits him, and he can be devious and manipulative if he needs to be. He had access to your children since they were infants, and he is capable of colonising their young minds if he wants to do so. He can be persistent in the message that he wants to give your children, while couching it in reasonable terms. He can persuade them that you are not good enough, and that he carries the responsibility for the whole family. When your children hear raised voices or see you crying, he will persuade them that you are the cause of the row. He may convince them that nothing happened, and that you are being hysterical. Eventually, he may target one or more of your children to take sides with him, and to join in the condemnation of you.

Many psychephiles work persistently to groom some or all of your children to betray you. If you have teenage children, he may invite them to live with him, as he can give them freedom – and more money than you. He will use his access to criticise you and undermine your authority.

Most of these men are completely unaware of the damage they are doing to their children. The use of young minds and hearts as ammunition against a parent is devastating for the child, and splits his or her spirit. If a young mind is bombarded with lies about one of its parents, it becomes increasingly difficult for that child to make sense of the tension that it feels. The child may feel that the level of tension in the home is normal, and that the solution to the family's distress is simple. Like the target woman, the child may come to believe that the anxiety he or she experiences is due to their own inadequacy, and that it is up to them to cope with the distress.

Your children are also like you in that they may meet therapists, who believe they can empower the child to cope with and recover from the distress caused by the abuse of a parent. As with you, it is unhelpful to attempt any form of therapy while the child is still subjected to the abuse. The continued false hope raised by the therapist, and the continued powerful but subtle impact of the abuser, may convince the child that he or she is even more inadequate. The power of the abuser is to persuade the child that he is not being abusive but that he is behaving like any other father. The child becomes confused and anxious, and personalises the distress. Like you, what your child needs is the absence of further abuse. If this freedom is established, then the child can, if necessary, avail of help to explore what happened, and to verify the child's innate sense of right and wrong.

161

How can I help my children?

If the father of your children is a psychephile, he will be able to access your children in spite of you. Unless you can prove a serious level of child abuse, he will not be barred from them; most psychephiles are too clever to be found guilty of their crimes. If you do not obtain the protection of the court, you will be required to allow him access to your children. You are not in a position to protect your children from him: whether he lives with you or in another place, he can get into the minds of your children.

You may wish to provide a barrier between your partner and your children, but taking this position can be dangerous for you and unhelpful for your children. They may grow up believing that you should have shielded them, and may be more angry with you than with the abuser. The feelings of inadequacy that can arise from your helplessness can be compounded by the pleadings of your children for you to do something. They may even plead with you to concede to their father, so that the home will be less tense. Your children are unaware of the power imbalance between you and your abuser, and they see you both as equally adult and equally resourceful.

It is unhelpful for your children if you believe that they are unaffected by the abuse you are suffering, or that your children do not need to know how they are being manipulated. You cannot hide the tension that exists in your relationship, and most children will feel the strain of this tension. You cannot hide the noise of your arguments and the disrespect that you suffer from their father. This persistent low-level abuse is normalised by your children, and may become the yardstick by which they measure all intimate relationships. While this low-level mind-control is tolerated by many, because it ignores the process of coercion that underpins it, it may encourage the children to blame you when you plead for it to stop.

You are sucked into debates with your abuser over seemingly trivial issues, and you will be blamed for any escalation in tension. This tension may lead to a disproportionate level of anxiety in some of your children, which is internalised by some children into self-blame. This self-blame can arise from a child's belief that they should not be so upset, as the issue seems so trivial. A child may also take blame if he or she thinks that they did something to trigger the tension. For instance, if your abuser arrives home and begins to berate you about the state of the house or the fact that your children have not completed their homework or their chores, some of your children may feel guilt or shame for not having done what you asked them to do.

As I have already written, you will be able to react differently once you are alert to the tactics of your abuser; it is also possible that your children will resist blaming themselves or you, if they can get a clearer picture of what their father is doing.

As your children grow older, you can reveal the tactics that their father uses in a language that they understand. You can do this by relating their experiences to your own. It is best if you can make these revelations without judging or condemning their father. It is also essential that you assure them that you can cope with the abuser, and that you are in a position to hear how they are being influenced by him. Your children need to be told repeatedly that the stress they are feeling is legitimate, and that they are not alone in their anxiety. Unless your children are given the words to describe their embarrassment, anxiety, fear and anger, they may come to believe that they are alone in feeling these emotions. I have encountered many young men who have been unable to discuss these emotions because they were never given the words to explain them. I have met many young women who are familiar with the language of emotion and are better at describing their feelings. Of course, plenty of young men are in touch with their feelings, and many young women are not. I would encourage you to talk about these feelings to your son in a language that will encourage him to explore the various elements that comprise his emotional world. A young boy has a rich emotional life, and if this is ignored he may grow up into a young man who channels all his emotions into anger.

Being emotionally available to your children as they grow up is extremely difficult if your mind is dominated by your abuser. Although you may be reluctant to try to unwind his brainwashing for your own sake, you might find the motivation to do so because of your desire to be a good mother. This motivation can help you clarify your thinking and go back to giving an intuitive response to your children. When your children are teenagers, they will benefit most from your intuition. Your instinctive responses will allow you to maintain some structure in their lives. You will need to avoid explaining your decisions, as your children will be expert at picking holes in your reasoning. Relying on intuition with your children will also encourage you to use it more often in your adult world. This repeated use in relation to immediate issues will help you make instinctive decisions about the bigger issues in your life.

Will he ever change?

This may be a question that will bother you long after you have stopped living with your abuser. The answer can be divided into two parts. Will he change his behaviour? Maybe. Will he change his sense of entitlement? Unlikely.

If you can accept that his behaviour is intentional, then you will understand that he has a vast range of tactics that he can use to help him target, set up and groom a new partner. Whereas he may be rude and aggressive to you, so that you concede to him, he may be polite and charming to his next partner, if this approach is likely to be more successful with her. He measures his success by finding the path of least resistance when it comes to achieving his goals. Ultimately, he wants to have a partner who will be available to him sexually when it suits him. You may have been seduced initially by his charms and his reassurances, but if you are unhappy with him, it is probably because you were forced to allow him to dictate the level of intimacy between you. You may never have said 'no' because you knew that you would endure constant pressure until you gave in to him. You may have pleaded for some autonomy and could only achieve that position when you left his bed. Or you may have longed for physical intimacy but been rejected.

Getting a new partner who would acknowledge his sexual priority without resistance might allow the psychephile to behave in a completely different manner in any new relationship. He might become less demanding about smaller issues, and less critical of the woman's behaviour or lifestyle; he might even begin to compliment her on her efforts. He has denied you any of this pleasantness because he is afraid of losing control over you. He may not require any of these tactics to establish and maintain control of his new partner, as she may be willing to accept his terms and conditions from the outset.

He may also adapt his tactics if the new target-woman establishes some redline issues from the outset of the relationship. She may convince him that if he behaves in certain ways, she would leave him immediately. He may respect her boundaries, but he will only do so if he can establish his primacy in some other way. You may eventually be told that he does not behave in the angry, aggressive or violent ways that you experienced. You may learn that his behaviour is different, or that he seems to have mellowed. This information may make you sad or angry: you will regret that he was not like that with you. It may be hard for you to accept, but the real change is that the woman he is with can be successfully manipulated by means of different tactics. These changes are superficial, and are indicators that he can achieve his aims more successfully using other tactics.

His behaviour may change, but his sense of entitlement will remain intact, or may even be enhanced by his ability to gain control over another target-woman. Very few men diminish this sense of entitlement, as it is the bedrock of their sexual identity, and will remain with them from the onset of puberty until they die. They may eventually lose the ability to be sexually active, but they will remain convinced that women are lesser beings and are there to serve them. The development of pharmaceutical methods to slow the onset of impotence has been a positive development in many loving relationships, but may have prolonged the distress for the partners of psychephiles. A client of mine wanted to know if her seventy-four-year-old husband could be affected by inhaling the fumes emitted by a plant they had in their house, as he had recently become very demanding in bed. It subsequently emerged that this psychephile, who had subjected his wife and children to a life of abuse and violence, was buying pills on the internet but blaming the fumes for his new-found vigour. His wife, who suffered from several painful conditions related to her advancing age, was not allowed to reject him when he wanted sex.

Does his new partner know what he is like?

The man who seduced you into starting a long-term intimate relationship with him is a clever, devious, single-minded and malevolent person. It is unlikely that you knew any of this about him, as he kept these personality traits hidden from you when you first met. He invaded your mind and colonised your thoughts without you knowing what he was doing. He used whatever smoke-screen worked best to hide his real intentions. He may have persuaded you to feel sorry for him and invited you to care for him. He may have convinced you that he was a 'winner' and that you were privileged to have him as a partner. He may even have convinced you that the two of you would make a great team and that, if you stuck together, you could achieve your dreams. Some of his tactics worked; even though your instincts may have made you feel unsure, you ignored any warning signs and committed to the relationship. What was certain was that you did not really know the man that you were living with. On reflection, you may admit that, having shared his bed for years, you still do not know much about who he really is.

His new partner may be in a worse position than you. Along with all the tactics he may have used on you, she will also be seduced into having pity for him. This pity will be fuelled by the stories he will tell her of his relationship with you, and how you let him down, in spite of his best efforts to please you. If you have children together, he may persuade her that you are also punishing him by turning his children against him. He may tell her that he tried his best to control your spending or your drinking, but that you ignored him. He may tell her of the hurt and anguish he felt when he found out you were having an affair. Whatever range of tactics he used when he met you will be enhanced by his ability to present himself as the victim of your relationship, and will be used effectively to deflect any concerns that the new partner might have about him.

In some cases, the psychephile may be driven by his own arrogance into a new relationship, where he may believe in his own entitlement without taking the steps to establish it in the mind of his new partner. This arrogance may encourage him to act in ways that his new partner will never accept. Without being able to explain herself, the woman may leave the relationship, even though she cannot fully rationalise her decision. Without knowing him, her intuition can inform her that he is not good for her, and she may separate from him. I have met some women who had been in relationships with the same psychephile: unless they have both been equally resistant, that means that they both resist in exactly the same way, and have had different experiences of the same man. If an abuser can establish his control without being intimidatory or violent, he may never frighten his partner. Many women have lived lives of quiet desperation without ever knowing that their partner is an abusive man.

Psychephiles behave differently in different circumstances and with different people. Spouses, children, colleagues, friends and even therapists will encounter different behaviours when they meet him. His talent is to hide his real self from the world. His hidden motivation is driven by a fear that we will find out that he is ordinary, and not the little god that he would like us to believe he is.

Why did you get caught again?

You may be like some of my clients, who have had more than one experience of abusive men. You may have left your first relationship because your abuser was unskilled and he had failed to establish his mind-control over you. I regard these men as under-developed psychephiles who are still practising the arts of coercive control. They have a series of short-term abusive relationships until they become expert in the required techniques. If you have escaped one or more of these trainee psychephiles, you may feel very angry with yourself for having got into a relationship with a full-fledged psychephile. You may think that you should have learned to recognise and avoid these abusers. This is unfair to you, because you were never aware of the tactics employed by any of your previous abusive partners. You may not be able to explain why you left these relationships, or stayed in your current one.

This lack of explanation is not your fault, but is a direct result of the persistent, destructive behaviours of all male intimate abusers. These men are all capable of building a smokescreen that hides their intentions. They are also very good actors, and can manipulate your emotions to suit themselves. They can make you feel sorry for them, or afraid of them; eventually, they can get you to feel both of these emotions at the same time. They will dismantle your emotional barriers and invade your emotional life. You will lose control of your emotions, and he will be able to dictate how you feel internally, even though you may try to hide your feelings from everybody. You will have little or no private life, but you will not know how you lost your integrity.

Because you are not aware of the control process, you can escape from one trainee psychephile and still end up with an expert psychephile. He may also have had some experience of intimate relationships, as he developed his skills: he was able to target, set up and groom you in a way that was different from the way in which your previous partners had done. This skill means that you were seduced without you knowing it; the reason it happened to you is that he decided to target you. He did so by using the usual tactics, but skilfully applied these tactics in ways that were new to you.

When you are free

Many clients describe their journey to freedom as like moving towards a light at the end of a tunnel. They talk about making a little progress sometimes and then being pulled back, or they see the light as being closer and then moving further away. This stop-start journey seems very slow, and they feel guilty about not being able to move forward with greater speed. You may even notice that when you are no longer sharing his bed or his home, you can still be upset by his lies and manipulations. The tunnel can seem endless, and the journey can appear to be on an incline that becomes progressively steeper. You may feel that your energy is becoming depleted, and that you are beginning to despair of ever reaching the light. You may be anxious that you have taken the wrong path and that, instead of making progress, you are going round in circles.

I prefer if you think about your journey in a different way. Instead of seeing the light of freedom as a distant objective, I would encourage you to imagine that the light is inside your head. This light is clouded by the confusion he has generated; it will become brighter as soon as you clear this confusion.

When you have cleared the fog in your mind, you will realise that you are now in the light, and that the clarity is unfamiliar but, hopefully, also exciting. Being in an unfamiliar space may cause you some anxiety; this is why I would like you to have regained confidence in your intuition. This renewed confidence will allow you to make decisions that are in your best interests. I remind you again that I encourage you to consider making very small changes initially. I suggest that you begin to stop explaining your decisions to others. Your family or friends will find it difficult to understand your actions, as they will not see the need for the mental journey that you are undertaking.

The benefits of this slow unravelling of his mind-control may be that you will identify the range of tactics that have been used, and probably continue, to be used on you. This process of identification will be useful in locating the problems solely with your abuser, and help you free yourself of the guilt and blame which you have been forced to carry. The light that you are seeing, and the clarity with which you view your abuser, will allow you to develop your future plans with the confidence and certainty that you need in order to live a contented life.

Part 4

Some Concluding Thoughts about Abusers

A new definition of partner abuse

Adult intimate abuse is a process of seduction and coercion, founded on mind-control, by which an abuser establishes and maintains dominance over the partner.

I am confident that the principal reason that intimate abuse remains an endemic problem in our society is because we have failed to define the problem. The literature accurately describes the effects of the problem on the people who are targeted by the abuser, but ends the description there. This approach has resulted in the community focusing its attention on the target-person, while the abuser remains hidden. Taking the focus away from the abuser allows him to manipulate our response and invites us to locate part of the blame on you. Ultimately, they create the problem and direct our response to it. Within the last ten years, there has been some stretching of the definition of intimate abuse, but we, the community of helpers and researchers, have retained the same focus, which fails to define what the abuser does. I want to propose a new definition, which will help us all, helpers and targets alike, to uncover the behaviour of the abusive partner. I hope to define the abuser in terms of how they treat their target partner.

What has been missing in our analysis of intimate abuse is the fact that people who manage to set up and maintain a long-term abusive relationship do so by initially taking control of the thoughts and emotional reactions, and subsequently behaviour, of the target-person. This process, which goes on during the targeting, setting up and grooming of the target-person, will underpin the abuser's ability to manage and maintain their dominant position within the relationship. In other words, the tactics of control and coercion are enacted during the very first steps of the relationship, sometimes even before the target-person would describe the relationship as having started.

The abuser who uses these tactics will not admit to them, as they are only of value if they remain hidden. The target is unaware of them, and so is unable to describe them. Academics and practitioners have been slow to recognise these tactics, but the effects of the brainwashing have been known for some time. In a literature review, I have found that Jones (2000) wrote about women who were brainwashed without acknowledging how or why it happened. In separate books published in 2010, the authors Itzin and Nicolson, while dealing with mental health and psychology, make no reference to mind-control or brainwashing. Itzin et al (2010) continue to define adult intimate abuse as 'the physical, sexual, emotional and/or financial abuse of people who are or have been intimate partners . . . in order to maintain power and control over that person'. Nicolson (2010) says that contemporary definitions are unequivocal, and quotes from the Shelter website: 'Domestic abuse is when someone close to you (usually your spouse, partner, ex-spouse or ex-partner) behaves towards to you in a way that causes physical, mental or emotional damage. It need not necessarily be physical violence.'

I have explored these definitions, and the process of stretching these definitions, as described by Evan Stark (2007). In his introduction, Stark states that the 'key finding is that the domestic violence revolution appears to have had little effect on coercive control, the most widespread and devastating strategy men use to dominate women in personal life'. Stark and Donald Dutton (2006) have tried to encompass some of the lacunas in our interventions in this area by suggesting new approaches and developing new theories. Stark suggests that we need to dig deeper and broaden the discussion, and says that we need to avoid recording individual acts without explaining their impact in the context of an intimate relationship. He suggests that this approach is 'once again depicting the bars without grasping that they are part of a cage'.

Dutton (2006) states that 'research and policy in domestic violence are at a critical crossroads' and that 'present practices are not working'. He also states that 'to remain closed-minded at this juncture may make one a faithful ideologue but it does no service to the victims of intimate partner violence'.

While these working definitions have been developed over many years, they fail to include the initial tactics of targeting, setting up and grooming, which are the essential foundations of control. These definitions also fail to explain why someone who comes into the relationship with a strong sense of power, in the physical, emotional and financial spheres, would need to engage in the energetic pursuit of more power. What I have learned from working with both male abusers and their female victims is that all the efforts of the male offender are focused on getting and maintaining sexual power, which is the one area where the woman has an equality of power at the beginning of the relationship. What I mean by this is that most men have the capacity to satisfy their own financial, emotional and physical needs. They are usually strong enough, clever enough and socially accepted enough, to make their own way in the world. They may see an extra benefit to their own image if a wife and children surround them, but they do not have the power to have their sexual needs met without negotiation.

Initially, the male abuser will aim to seduce the target-woman. Having achieved sexual intimacy, he will increase his control until the woman is bereft of her sexual integrity and he controls the level, frequency and type of activities connected to their intimate lives. This control may also entitle him in his eyes, to engage in sexual activity outside of his long-term intimate relationship. In some cases, it can reassure him that any sexual deviancy on his part will probably remain hidden.

Dutton (2006) says that many of the later assessment scales assess outcomes as well as abuse and violence. He agrees that it is difficult to distinguish in language a 'push' which results in somebody being moved sideways and a 'push' which results in somebody falling downstairs. He also admits that the definition that he uses is chosen 'with a view to intervention'. This choice results in an attempt to define intimate abuse as a precise behaviour on a continuum of violent and abusive behaviours which are recognised by most criminal-justice systems. I would like to propose that the effect of any abusive action cannot be measured by its physical effects, but by the enforcement of control that even the most minor of abuses can achieve when the power differential is already established. Thus a hand on a target partner's shoulder can be as terrifying as a punch in the face for an individual who is already under the mental control of the intimate abuser. Also, I believe that instead of trying to fit our definition into the current criminal-justice language, we need to move the justice system to view intimate abuse as a very different process.

The impact of the initial hidden mind-control makes it difficult for us to appreciate the effect of any known incident of intimidation or violence. Because it has remained hidden from the community, we are drawn into a debate about physical assaults between men and women and, increasingly, between any two partners in an intimate relationship (man-man and woman-woman). There is no comparison between being physically assaulted by someone who is stronger than you and being raped by someone who says they love you. While many couples struggle to get on, a person whose spirit is being eroded is in danger of losing their integrity. I believe that if I meet a person, either man or woman, who is being brainwashed in their intimate relationship, my duty is to alert them to the process, and to protect them from further manipulation and mind-control.

While the definition of intimate abuse is, according to Stark, in need of stretching, I would like to suggest that a more effective definition is one that focuses on the perpetrator. A new definition needs to incorporate the initial tactics of mind-control and seduction, which happen covertly at the initiation of the relationship, and the reasons for their use. This description might help all of us to define more accurately the experience of the target-person and better inform the legal system about the practices of the abuser. This definition would run: *Adult intimate abuse is a process of seduction and coercion, founded on mind-control, by which an abuser establishes and maintains dominance over the partner. Continued abuse is possible, and maintained, by the abusive person's persistent and effective lying, denying, and re-directing of blame.*

I have developed this working definition over the last twenty years, while engaging with target-women, abusers, academic researchers and front-line practitioners. Having searched the literature for answers, I have also found that this definition is the most useful when it comes to explaining the pervasive, near-obsessive preoccupation of the target-person, their inability to get the abuser off their mind and out of their lives, and their difficulty to be believed, with a view to making society hold the abuser accountable.

This definition, which is very different from the ones currently in use in Ireland and throughout Europe, may help us understand the fundamental covert tactics and intentions that the offender uses, and which are unknown to the target and undeclared by the abuser. It may also help us to begin to realise why all the energy and expertise expended over the last sixty years could result in Stark (2000) declaring that the revolution which was initiated by abusive women has stalled, and for many current writers to proclaim that intimate abuse continues to be endemic in all levels of society.

The definition is not an attempt to fit the crime into our criminal-justice system, but is designed to encourage our justice system to re-think its approach to intimate violence. We may have moved on from what Dutton (2006) calls the age of denial, but we have done so while failing to identify what is really going on. We have responded to the voice of the abuser as spoken by their target. These accounts of abuse and violence have not captured the covert behaviours that the skilled offender has used to establish and maintain control. Because we have failed to identify and define these behaviours, we have attempted to solve the problem before we know what is really happening. If we acknowledge the covert tactics of targeting, setting up and grooming, which are the foundations of all long-term abusive relationships, we, as a community, may begin to develop a more focused and effective intervention strategy.

This new definition and intervention strategy will then inform the way in which we, the helpers and protectors of our society, approach the people involved in an abusive relationship. We will need to change the way in which we have tried to analyse the abuser's behaviour in the light of their initial tactics. We will find that our psychological definitions and explanations of intimate abuse and violence do not capture the deliberate methods used by the abuser to establish this control. We will need to re-examine the various strategies and interventions, individual and group, which have proven to be of little use up to now. As Dutton (2006) says, treatment is not working, and activists who really want to diminish the incidence of domestic violence have to abandon outmoded ways of thinking about the problem.

Why a thorough description of the behaviour of the skilled abuser is necessary

I suggest that we, helpers and protectors, examine our approach to any woman or man who is the target of these tactics and behaviours. I suggest that the power of the mind-control and seduction is acknowledged. The initial tactics of the abuser gives them a strength that goes far beyond what has been recognised up to now. If we begin to measure the power of mind-control and seduction employed by the abuser, we will find it difficult to continue to blame the target-person for her experience – and that, in turn, will make a major impact on the target's self-blaming. We may begin to recognise that when target-women are available to their abusers, they are unable to think straight, and that all our conversations with them are filtered through the voice of the abuser, which the targets carry in their heads. While the person looking for our help is listening to us, they may also be listening to their abuser, and if that abuser has established control, the target will find it hard to hear what we say. This means that instead of trying to win the target-person over, we will be more effective if we establish a mental refuge for them, where the abuser's voice is reduced or eliminated.

The experience of far too many abused women who have attempted to get help from the community is that they have been judged, blamed, and seen as a problem for the social services. This is the inevitable result of their revelations about difficulties in the relationship. The eyes of the community of helpers become solely focused on the abused person, while the abuser remains hidden. This failure to acknowledge the abuser's initial tactics of mind-control has resulted in the abusers being confirmed in their own sense of entitlement. It has also resulted in the abused person being afraid of the help being offered, as they know we are all missing something but are unable to explain to us what we are missing. They can feel the effects of being set up and groomed, but are unable to describe what happened, or how. These missing ingredients are the mind-control that the abusers achieve while they appear to be loving, and the skilful lying of which they are capable. Without these ingredients, the target-person would instinctively know that the behaviour is wrong, and that they do not deserve to be abused, and the rest of society would immediately recognise the abuse for what it is, and locate the blame accordingly.

The issue of focusing on target experience

Some day, the research community might end up with a term that covers all the behaviours (and their effects) of an intimate abuser. This is not to medicalise or explain the behaviour, but to describe actions that can be recognised. It should not be seen as an attempt to excuse the deliberate agenda of control, and the subsequent efforts to avoid sanction. Recognising the lack of a comprehensive psychological terminology, my aim is to be concise and distinctive in identifying the various aspects of destructive behaviour that are employed by the abuser to assert and maintain his dominance.

This description of the skilled abuser will help us to concentrate on his behaviour. It will demand that we resist making excuses for the perpetrator or feeling sorry for him. It will also focus on his present and future behaviour, and not fall into the trap of analysing his past in order to justify his current decisions. While the description will be of benefit to us, the observers, it will be invaluable to the family who are caught up in this nightmare. The target woman will have a clearer picture of the man with whom she is living. She will begin to realise the real strength of the forces with which she is grappling. She may begin to appreciate that the person who shares her bed is beyond her sphere of influence, and is impervious to her requests or pleadings. This realisation will help her to take the focus away from her own responsibilities and allow her to examine his behaviour in a new light. As she does so, she may become less available to his mental control of her, and may regain some of the instinctive analysis she had before she met him.

The children of the couple will also benefit from an accurate diagnosis of the problem, as it will give them an explanation for the level of tension between their parents. It can also be used to help the children avoid being used as ammunition or buffers by their parents. The black-and-white thinking which is the gift of young people allows them to come to a clear decision about what is right and wrong about the behaviour of their parents. The language of the diagnosis may need to be simplified for them, but it is startling how quickly eight-year-olds can make clear judgement calls about bad behaviour. There is little doubt that children caught up in the intrigue of an intimate abuser are very vulnerable to fear and mind-control. It is vital for these children that their experiences are identified and explained in an accurate way. It is also essential that the abuse is identified and stopped before an abusive father is allowed to use child access as a further means of partner abuse. Any man who abuses the mother of his children cannot be regarded as a good parent.

The description may also be the one hope the abuser has of redeeming himself. By having a mirror held up to him, the offender may recognise the reality of his behaviour. He may see for the first time the true extent of his deviousness and arrogance. Confronted with this reality, he will be unable to transfer the blame to others, or to pretend that his behaviour is accidental or beyond his control. If he is sanctioned in a way that accepts no minimisation, and acknowledges his true intentions, he may be given an insight into the reality of his entitlement. Any other approach will allow him to dodge his reality, and will inevitably result in his continuing abusive behaviours.

In order to make an effective and accurate assessment, we will need a certain amount of information. If we can establish that the target-woman has been subjected to the tactics of targeting, setting up and grooming, we can assume that her partner may be a skilled abuser. If the woman includes his thinking in her analysis, we can be fairly sure that she is subject to mind-control. This control may be seen if the client is invited to make a small change to her routine, and she states vehemently that he would not approve of the change. We can learn more by exploring the certainty with which the woman replies to the small request, and seeking out the genesis of that certainty. We may learn a little of how she came to know that change could be dangerous for her, and that resistance to his instructions would not be tolerated.

The methods used by skilled abusers vary. Some of them increase the mental anguish of the woman until she accedes to his demands. Others may revert to aggression and violence to attain their goals. But they will all manage to get what they want, and to avoid any sanction. To get an accurate measure of what the man is doing, we need to examine the effect on the woman rather than the detail of his behaviour. What we will probably find is that all women are controlled to the same extent, even though some abusers use different tactics. If the target-woman has been manipulated into following his demands, he has used effective and similar tactics on her for some time. The belief that some abusers are more dangerous than others belies that fact that they can all be lethal unless they get what they want.

Don Hennessy

The information given by the target-woman can be enhanced by others. International best estimates claim that women approach many people and agencies for help without revealing the reality of their lives. Family, friends, workmates, hairdressers and teachers may have some knowledge that the woman is being abused. Doctors, social workers, clergy and solicitors may also have pieces of information which can influence a diagnosis. Police and judges may already be involved with the family. Each individual or agency may have only a small piece of information about the abuse, but when all this collateral information is brought together, a clearer picture will emerge about the problem, and its source.

The issue of lying and redirecting blame

Most professionals that I have met over the last number of years who encounter the perpetrators or the victims of domestic violence have been shocked to realise that they have little or no training in dealing with dishonesty. They seem to believe that people are intrinsically truthful and that, if they say something that is not true, it is not done deliberately. This naivety gives the skilled abuser a huge advantage over a victim who tries to tell the truth. Because the professional is lacking training in working with liars, because he or she is unaware of the agenda of the abuser, the professional becomes a victim too. He or she is groomed into siding with the abuser while attempting to be non-judgemental and fair. This results in unintended collusion by the professional with the abuser. Judges, barristers, solicitors, police and social workers have all been groomed by some of the abusers we have met. Psychiatrists, psychologists and doctors have all failed to recognise or challenge the lies that abusers have told them. Counsellors and psychotherapists have berated me for not showing 'unconditional positive regard' towards men who are trying to manipulate me. Supporters, family and friends of our clients have failed to locate the responsibility of the abuse on the shoulders of the actual abuser. If we had a solid, effective way of detecting the abuser's lies and re-direction of blame, we would be able to uncover the abusive behaviour and hold the abuser responsible.

This absence of a clear and understandable description of the skilled abuser inevitably means that he can distract us from his behaviour and his intentions. He can effortlessly switch our focus away from him and onto the victim, or onto circumstances over which he has no control. He can groom any professional into feeling sorry for him. He does this mainly by switching the conversation away from anything that might be seen as a challenge to his position. This grooming will inevitably result in an inaccurate diagnosis both of the man and of the source of the problem. He will present a range of symptoms, which will encourage us to label him as depressed, damaged from childhood experiences, traumatised by recent or current events, or overwhelmed by personal stress. He may also try to convince us of his social immaturity, his inability to communicate, his jealousy or his paranoia.

If he fails to groom us into labelling him as lacking or as being over-responsible – in other words, if he fails to have us accept his self-centred explanations – he will try to have us focus on issues outside himself. He will want to us to accept that he has a 'short fuse', which he would want us to believe is beyond his control. He will have a long list of issues about his partner, which, separately or collectively, will be presented as valid reasons for his bad behaviour. He may also include his unruly children, his lack of social outlets, his high-pressure job, or his commitment to his family of origin as excuses for his abusive behaviour.

Because most professionals want to see the good in people, and want to feel that they can be of help to the family, it suits them that we still have no accurate way of identifying the skilled abuser. This lack of an accurate diagnosis of the malevolence of these men allows the professionals to feel superior and capable. They feel superior because many of them believe themselves to be better at self-control, even though they share some of the experiences of the abuser. Professionals in every agency tend to put skilled abusers into a category where they can be managed and helped. Many professionals also fail to see the unique context of the abuse, and the extraordinary power that the abuser uses to hide his responsibility.

The lack of an accurate diagnosis will also mean that the abuser may be given a symptom-focused explanation of his behaviour. He may be labelled as depressed as a result of living with an uncooperative partner, or as a result of his anxiety regarding the future of the family. He seldom makes contact with social services until his partner is suggesting that they split up, and he can give a compelling account of the reasons why she should be encouraged to stay. He will persuade the professional of his good intentions, and will direct the diagnosis into the area of his depression. He may even present himself as paranoid, and be diagnosed accordingly.

He may manoeuvre the professional into accepting that he is under personal stress because of financial pressure, or because of some issue relating to his physical health. This tactic invites the professional to feel pity for him, and to admire his commitment and determination to keep his relationship and family intact. He can plead that he is unsupported, and that his partner is very difficult to live with. I have had good women described as drunks, spendthrifts or whores – and sometimes all three – by abusers who are seeking my sympathy. I have been invited to agree that, if I was living with one of these women, I would also be abusive and violent.

The most effective tactic that an abuser uses when he encounters a therapist or social worker is to present himself as a victim of childhood trauma. The sympathy that this evokes can allow the professional to create an explanation and an excuse for the person's current abuse. It can invite the therapist or social worker into an attempt to understand the man in the same way as the target-woman has already been invited to do. Most of his story is exaggerated, and some of it may be complete fiction, but his convincing demeanour and flawless lying will convince the professional that he or she has found the source of the problem. It is inevitable that such a diagnosis will allow the professional to feel both competent and hopeful.

Sadly, this unprofessional diagnosis will result in the target-woman being ignored or blamed, and the abuse tolerated. Once the skilled abuser has managed to obtain a diagnosis that excuses himself and blames his partner or his history, he feels vindicated, and more convinced than ever of his sense of entitlement. He becomes more demanding and more forceful if he is resisted. He can become even more arrogant, as he is encouraged by his ability to manipulate the system. Therapists, social workers, lawyers and judges may eventually encounter his arrogance, and may be groomed into supporting him.

This support is turned by the skilled abuser into collusion. He uses the fact that all these people are on his side to further undermine the position of the woman, until she eventually feels hopeless and abandoned by society. He shuts off her supports and challenges her authority. He dictates her behaviour and threatens dire consequences for disobedience. Indications of being impoverished, suggestions of losing her children, and threats to kill are now supported by the realisation for the woman that he might get away with these threats because of his inaccurate diagnosis. Her life becomes more difficult, her hope is diminished, and the confidence and self-belief of the abuser are enhanced by the lack of an accurate and helpful diagnosis.

The pathology that drives the behaviour of the man remains undetected. Though the woman feels the effects of his pathology, she is unable to identify it in psychological terms, and is reluctant to talk about it. She knows that what he is doing is not right, but she blames herself or accepts his excuses. The agencies that meet the family also feel the force of his abusive tactics, and his unrelenting drive to maintain his control. This unrelenting drive is the force that we encounter if we attempt to gain access to his real self. It is the force that calls on the woman to admit that, even after years of apparent intimacy, she knows very little of his inner world. It is the force that threatens us or grooms us into giving a superficial diagnosis of his behaviour. It directs us to draw issues of history and circumstance into our thinking. It is the shield by which his real self remains hidden from us. This shield makes him immune to our directions and allows him to continue to abuse and violate his partner.

In sum, we can break down the separate and obvious issues of the abuse into two categories.

1. Physical and psychological abuse

The level of identifiable behaviour, which begins to emerge as we explore the relationship, has a profound effect on our response. The idea that an apparently normal and respectful man would threaten and assault the woman who is trying to love him can be very difficult to accept. It may also be hard for us to accept that the access he gains to her thinking gives him an extraordinary base from which to weave his influence. The realisation that a man would regard his partner as sexually inferior, that he would feel entitled to be sexually dominant, connects with our own ambivalence about sexual priority.

These abuses, including mind-control, intimidation, physical assault and rape, can all be documented in a way that presents a compelling body of evidence for use in criminal proceedings. But without a legal revolution, this level of evidence will remain unnoticed and ignored. The discussion becomes one of what he did in a known incident, and what her role was in the same incident. The judgement then ignores the context of an intimate relationship and grades the violence as being slight or rare, by putting it on the same scale as stranger violence. This process allows the man to manipulate the system by declaring that his behaviour was out of character for him, or that he will not repeat the crime.

It would be much more effective if, instead of analysing what he did, we found a way of measuring the effect of his behaviour on his partner. Skilled abusers have a range of physical and psychological tactics that they use to achieve their aims, so that while they may use different behaviours, the effects on the various target-women is the same. This is evident whether the woman is from Ireland or from elsewhere in Europe, or from anywhere else in the world. The fact is that all abused women are mind-controlled and degraded. Abused women feel unheard throughout the world, not because they have not spoken, but because they have not been believed.

2. Pathological denial and hostile paranoia

When we try to help a couple, we are burdened by our inability fully to believe the depth of control and abuse that has already been established by the skilled abuser. We are also stymied by the intense level of denial, which is designed to be impervious to the truth. The abuser will distract us, and misdirect us, with subtle changes in his conversation. If we continue to pursue him, we will encounter a well-developed paranoia that can allow him to threaten and intimidate us.

This combination of lying and fearful manipulation becomes the shield behind which the skilled abuser remains unreachable. Even if we accumulate all the evidence, and accurately challenge the man, we will find his shield impenetrable, and our influence negligible. The shield is designed to protect the abuser from experiencing any sanction for his actions. It is so successful that very few men are brought before the courts, and even fewer of them are convicted or sentenced. The durability of his constant lying allows him to ignore any reasonable intervention from social services. Social workers are continually frustrated, not by violence and abuse, but by the solid combination of denial and paranoia that blocks their interventions. Experienced social workers know this, and admit to avoiding the skilled abusers if possible. This is the primary reason why social workers generally hold the mothers accountable for the safety of their children. It is not just that they blame the mothers, but is also an implicit acknowledgement that engagement with the skilled abuser is unhelpful at best, and frightening at worst. Skilled abusers throughout the world remain unrepentant not because they have not been challenged but because they have disarmed every challenger.

The lack of an accurate diagnosis of the behaviour, the covert manipulation and the motivation of all male intimate abusers also results in the abuse being downgraded to a family conflict. The abuse is seen as part of a relationship dynamic that is prevalent in most intimate relationships. It is spoken of as a disagreement that got out of hand, and is accepted as unusual in terms of the normal level of conflict between the partners. It eventually becomes an issue of his word against hers; as his word is designed to groom his listeners, he usually emerges as the winner in front of the law, or in front of family and friends.

Therapists have told me that they have worked through repeated sessions where the man is verbal and convincing, and the woman is quiet and reticent. I have been told that these women need to motivate themselves and to take a more active role in the process of therapy. Therapists have also told me that they have worked with couples where the abuser is quiet and reasonable, and the woman is loud and expressive. I have had these women diagnosed as borderline personalities by counsellors who are not qualified to do so. Both of these interventions ignore the reality and the power of the man's behaviour.

Professionals who work with abusers and their partners continually fail to expose the underlying dynamic of the abuse and mind-control, and are inevitably groomed into supporting the abuser. Without an accurate description of the covert tactics of targeting, setting up and grooming, these therapists have no reason to do otherwise.

The lack of an accurate and detailed diagnosis of the skilled abuser will result in the downgrading of any evidence that has already been gathered by other professionals in the system. The paranoid denial of the abuser will cause any professional to accept the assessment of the abuser that he is not a violent man. This assessment may be arrived at in spite of historical and collateral information that the man has been abusive in the past. A prominent celebrity is today on the front pages of a national newspaper claiming that he is not a violent man, while admitting to pushing his partner. His partner is photographed with severe facial injuries and is alleging that it is not the first time that she has suffered injuries to her head. The response of many on social media seems to be one of sympathy for the abuser, as this publicity may damage his business and ruin his acting career. The feeling is that the woman went too far. If she had not been in a relationship with the abuser, if she did not have two children with him, if she was a customer of his business or a stranger on the street, he would now be facing charges of GBH (grievous bodily harm). Present indications are that a prosecution is unlikely. Even with a criminal conviction, the target-woman may be obliged to cooperate with her abuser in allowing him access to their children. I am unaware of any other court procedure where the judiciary do not insist on being given a detailed history of the defendant's criminality towards the victim before making a decision.

The perpetrator of male intimate abuse is stubborn and defiant. When I worked with groups of abusers, I grew to admire the exceptional ability they had to maintain their stated position. They could engage in long-winded conversations about their behaviour or attitude, and not move an inch from their self-centred beliefs. They used a number of tactics to protect themselves, two of the most prominent being repetition and distraction. I have listened to men who talk incessantly but are just repeating their preferred position. They can state their mantra that they are not violent men in many different ways. This ability to keep repeating their position is very effective. I now encourage any abused woman who is going to court to keep repeating that the only reason they are before the judge is to obtain the protection of the court for herself and her children. By repeating this mantra, they may avoid being traumatised by the lies being introduced by the abuser.

If the abuser wishes, he may also deal with a challenging conversation by introducing topics that are designed to distract from his behaviour. They can turn any risky conversations into one of victim-blaming, or of a traumatic childhood or of emotional anxiety. Engaging in any discussion of these topics will result in the questioner being sabotaged and frustrated. I have spoken to therapists and other professionals who eventually wilt from the pathological but relentless defiance of the skilled abuser.

The accurate and clear description of the skilled abuser is like the examination of a tumour that causes colon cancer. Without examining the tumour, we end up dealing with the effects, namely the pain, bleeding and diarrhoea. We try to solve the problem by working backwards from the symptoms to the solutions. Sadly, unlike the cancerous tumour, we are unable to treat the skilled abuser with chemotherapy or surgery. Unlike the tumour, the abuser is resistant to normal therapies, and is unable to accept that his actions are wrong or his entitlement is unjustified. A thorough description of his tactics will be akin to dissecting the tumour and uncovering how and why it works. It will also be a way of eliminating victim-blaming.

The thorough description will allow agencies and other professionals to develop systems and structures that will result in each case being managed impeccably. It will demand a level of inter-agency cooperation which is far beyond existing efforts in this area. It will inform the legal system of the possibilities of being groomed, and will oblige the same agencies to resist such a process. It will expose and explain some of the reasons why our systems are failing, and it will demonstrate that the skilled abuser is presently in charge of our response. It will indicate that we are all being compromised, and that our ambivalence and tolerance is being manipulated in favour of the male abuser. It will challenge society's view of marital rape, and expose our lack of a clear definition of consent. These gaps in our response will inevitably be closed if we are aware of the ability of the skilled abuser to avoid sanction. The diagnosis will eliminate our ability to minimise the issue, and will call on the justice system to protect women and children.

The new systems and structures can be based on compiled evidence, and can be monitored to develop responses which hold the skilled abuser to account. In Ireland, we lag behind other developed countries in our response to partner violence, while our politicians hide behind a constitution which was composed by men of property at a time when women had few rights. It was also influenced by a church that treated women as second-class citizens and demanded that they accede to their husband's sexual demands. These systemic failures have produced generations of men who are sexually arrogant, and women who are sexually demeaned. When we now have a clearer picture of these arrogant men, and a realisation that they treat all of us with disdain, we may begin to place them under a microscope. This detailed examination will give us a clear realisation of the forces we are up against, and may result in an innovative structure that will intervene effectively in the families of skilled abusers. This intervention needs to be effective and universal, so that our daughters will live lives that are satisfying, and our sons will resist a culture that might turn them into self-centred and uncaring partners.

The description will allow the family an opportunity to locate the problem, not within the family dynamic, but within the pathological behaviour of the abuser. It will become an essential aid in clarifying for the woman and her children the futility of their efforts to modify the man's behaviour. It will explain to the family why they have no role to play in his abuse, why their efforts to comply with his instructions may never be enough, and why they end up being blamed for their own distress. It will change the focus of the victims away from their own inadequacies and shine a spotlight on the unbelievable motivation and behaviour of the man. It will expose the tumour that is embedded in the family, and enable the other family members to examine this disease in a clear light. It is also likely that the community will put in place structures that will rescue the children of abusive fathers.

While the process of assessing and describing the skilled abuser is designed to develop methods of safety and protection for women in families, it is my fervent wish that it may also offer the first opportunity to reveal to the man the tactics and motivation attached to his destructive behaviour. This revelation must be done using accurate and understandable language that will be compelling and irresistible. This language will avoid the tactics of minimising and blaming which are the cornerstone of his defence, and expose to him the nature of his behaviour and the motivation behind it.

By exposing to the abuser the reality of his own behaviour, we are offering him an opportunity for contrition and redemption. He can become aware of the extent of his beliefs, his decision-making and his motivation, all which have driven his abusive behaviour. He can be invited to accept his responsibility and to grasp the reality of his arrogance and deviousness. He may even begin to accept the consequences of his actions, and admit that he is not entitled to dominate another person.

Without a clear and well-presented picture of his manipulation and of his cynical behaviours, he will remain engulfed in his sense of entitlement, and confirmed in his arrogance. This sense of arrogance will cause him to end up in emotional isolation, where he has no one to love him and few to tolerate him. No man should be alone, especially when the people who loved him withdrew from him because of his abusiveness. Presenting this reality takes courage, and an informed vision of what is really going on in a relationship. Not doing so is unfair to the man.

Bibliography

Bancroft, L. *Why Does He Do That?* (New York: Berkley Books, 2002)

Dutton, D. *Rethinking Domestic Violence* (Ottawa: University Press, 2006)

Hennessy, D. *How He Gets Into Her Head* (Cork: University Press, 2012)

Itzin et al. *Domestic and Sexual Violence and Abuse* (Abingdon: Routledge, 2010)

Jacobson, N. and Gottman, J. *Breaking the Cycle* (London: Bloomsbury Publishing, 1998)

Jones, A. *Next Time She'll Be Dead* (Boston: Beacon Press, 2000)

Nicolson, P. *Domestic Violence and Psychology* (Hove: Routledge, 2010)

Peck, M.S. *People of the Lie* (London: Arrow Books, 1990)

Stark, E. *Coercive Control* (New York: Oxford University Press, 2007)